Community
Capitalism

Lessons from Kalamazoo and Beyond

. . . .

RON KITCHENS
with DANIEL GROSS *and* HEATHER SMITH

AuthorHouse™
1663 Liberty Drive, Suite 200
Bloomington, IN 47403
www.authorhouse.com
Phone: 1-800-839-8640

AuthorHouse Revision: 07/22/2008
Original Edition: 04/2008

ISBN: 978-1-4343-8172-9 (sc)
      978-1-4343-8173-6 (dj)
      978-1- 4343-8174-3 (e)

Printed in the United States of America
Bloomington, Indiana

This book is printed on acid-free paper.

Dedicated to the

Community leaders who create a vision of prosperity;

Economic developers who daily succeed in implementing the vision;

And to the business men and women who create the wealth
that fuels the vision.

The best social program in the world
is a well-paying job with health care benefits
and a retirement program.

— EWING KAUFFMAN

CONTENTS

PREFACE
GRAB THE ROPE! XI

INTRODUCTION
SO WHAT IS COMMUNITY CAPITALISM? 1

CHAPTER ONE
PLACE: ROCKS, MARBLES AND SAND 9

CHAPTER TWO
CAPITAL: SHOW ME THE MONEY 27

CHAPTER THREE
INFRASTRUCTURE: BRICKS AND MORTAR 47

CHAPTER FOUR
TALENT: TALENT GETS IT DONE 65

CHAPTER FIVE
EDUCATION: THE PROMISE OF A BRIGHTER FUTURE 87

CONCLUSION
THE PIECES OF THE PUZZLE 103

EPILOGUE
COMMUNITY CAPITALISM 109

BLESSINGS

It has been said that success has many fathers and a project like this book is no different. Throughout the process, we have been blessed to have the assistance of many people we would like to thank. To those people who are quoted and not quoted in this book who took many, many hours to tell their stories, you warmed our souls with your commitment to changing the economic fortunes of people whose names you will probably never know.

This book could have never been written without the support of the Board of Directors of Southwest Michigan First: Bob Brown, John Brown, David Boyle, Craig DeNooyer, John Dunn, Mike Jandernoa, Bill Johnston, Don Parfet, Bill Parfet, Bill Richardson, Frank Sardone, Marilyn Schlack and Paul Spaude.

We thank our team members at Southwest Michigan First who dedicate themselves daily to the principles of Community Capitalism: Jill Bland, Jackie Nawrocki, Paul Neeb, Leslie Pawlak, John Plotnik and Megan Roschek.

We are deeply honored by the commitment of the team at Development Counsellors International, in particular Dariel Curren and Andy Levine, who served as not only mentors, prompters and counselors but also as great friends.

We would be remiss if we did not thank the people of Kalamazoo County, Michigan and beyond who seek a better future for all.

The authors would also like personally to thank:

Ron Kitchens: Lyn for reminding me about what is truly important, Kelsey for inspiring me to be better and my grandfather, John E. Williams, for encouraging me to write.

Dan Gross: The community leaders, executives and students of southwest Michigan, who gave so generously of their time to help me understand Kalamazoo's pioneering initiatives in Community Capitalism.

Heather Smith: The special people in the world who are brave enough to make a difference, are willing to take a chance, actually do what they say and share their gifts, whatever they may be, with the rest of us. A special thank you to my children, parents, friends who show unwavering support for me and the entire team at Southwest Michigan First.

GRAB THE ROPE!

"Grab the rope!"

That is what you are likely to hear if you find yourself on a ship, becalmed and threatened. That is what you will hear when you have no wind to sail by or engines to propel. You must resort to kedging to get out of trouble.

The act of kedging goes back as long as boats have traveled the water. Kedging is the act of having a light anchor (a kedge) loaded into a rowboat and taken out as far as the lines tied to it will allow. After dropping the anchor, every man, woman and child on the main boat grab the rope and pull the line as if his or her life depended on it, literally hauling the ship to the anchor. This is repeated again and again until the ship arrives at its destination or the fair winds once again blow.

This sounds like a lot of work. But if it is the only way to overcome a tide that is pulling you into the rocks, then doing the hard work yourself is the only choice.

This reminds me of where we now find ourselves in many communities around the nation. And like a ship's captain, we have a choice.

We can either decide to do the hard work and pull ourselves forward or we can hit the rocks, knowing that there will be casualties, but hoping that by a miracle some of us will survive.

We live in a time of psychological recession, a time when we hear every day about the bleakness of our future. We hear a lot about who is to blame for our economic lot in life. But we hear very little about what each of us can do to determine a path to a renewed future.

I believe that the future will not be written by those who believe we can no longer compete. Nor will it be written by those who would rather place blame or talk of partisan politics. The future will be written by those who grab the rope and pull the "ship" to prosperity.

I believe that prosperity looks a lot like the words of Ewing Kauffman who said, "The best social program in the world is a well-paying job with health care benefits and a retirement program." This is to say, that it will be businesses and individuals that will change our future, not government and politicians.

It will be people like you and me that will create the future. So, do as hundreds of people around you do every day...

GRAB THE ROPE!
Ron Kitchens, April 2008

INTRODUCTION:
SO WHAT IS COMMUNITY CAPITALISM?

Never doubt that a small group of
thoughtful committed citizens can change the world;
indeed, it's the only thing that ever has.

— MARGARET MEAD

It seems that these days, economic development is on everyone's lips. We are in a time when every political campaign – from a local city council race to the campaign for President of the United States – seems to focus on economic development and jobs. Who will ever forget the sign that hung in the 1992 campaign war room of then United States' presidential candidate Bill Clinton, which so eloquently stated, "It's the economy, stupid." Poetry, sheer poetry.

With all this focus, it's easy to believe that the spotlight on jobs and economic development is a modern phenomenon. Easy to believe, but wrong. Back in 190 B.C. when the first tax-free port, the Port of Delos, was declared, the Romans proclaimed it a tax haven for trade with the express purpose of growing its economy by diverting ships from the Port of Rhodes. Delos achieved its goal and Rhodes sank into insignificance. So, it can be said that people have been discussing AND practicing what is so commonly referred to as economic development for 2,200 years.

In the past few decades, we have seen economic development theories that focused on the Creative Class, Nerdistans, Gazelles, New Urbanism, Economic Gardeners, Tech Transfer, Innovators, Entrepreneurs and Smokestack Chasers. All of these economic theories have two things in common – they are all right and they are all wrong. That is also to say that as singular strategies for community and economic growth, they are not the sole solution; as components of a total strategy to grow a regional economy, they are correct.

The reality? Economic growth is a long-term strategy that requires the focused approach of key resources into five areas of a community. We call this approach Community Capitalism.

Innovation is the central issue in economic prosperity.

– MICHAEL PORTER

Community Capitalism approaches community growth as both a philanthropic and capitalist process that centers on investing a community's resources in a manner that ensures long-term economic success and relevancy. The five key areas of Community Capitalism are: Place, Capital, Infrastructure, Talent and Education. In order to successfully integrate Community Capitalism into an economy, all five areas must be addressed, not just one or two like the above-mentioned theories do. What's more, the concept must be embraced by an entire community in order for it to thrive.

Kalamazoo, Michigan is such a community. Its business climate is marked by a history rich in innovation and quality. The community has always taken pride in one very important thing – itself. And it has always considered one thing to be of the utmost importance – the community.

In order to understand how Kalamazoo became one of the purest examples of Community Capitalism, let's reflect on a brief history of its economy.

When a co-worker bemoaned to Dr. William E. Upjohn, founder of the pharmaceutical manufacturer Upjohn Company, that tablets were overtaking pills, he responded with equanimity, "Why yes, it is a big thing; but never mind, some day we shall have another big thing." For more than a century and a half, the town in which Upjohn built his company, Kalamazoo, saw one big thing come after another big thing. Optimism seemed a defining characteristic of Kalamazoo from its origin. Nationally renowned companies seemed to spring forward like crops in fields to be harvested.

Like virtually every other settlement in North America, Kalamazoo started as an agricultural settlement. When author James Fenimore Cooper visited in 1847, he found "the whole country was a wheat field." But as industrialization's roots spread throughout the Midwest, Kalamazoo's wheat fields were replaced by other things. For starters, the Kalamazoo Paper Company, formed in 1867, spawned a host of rivals and related firms, and by World War I, Kalamazoo was one of the largest paper producers in the world.

Concurrently in the late 19th century, celery became a huge industry. By 1900, some 4,000 acres were under cultivation and 400 celery farms employed 3,500 people. At about the same time, the A. M. Todd Company supplied about 90 percent of the world's supply of peppermint. And while few of the local buggy makers and early auto makers survived the transition from horse to car, the Checker Motors Corporation established Kalamazoo as home in the 1920s.

Two of the industrial acorns planted in Kalamazoo's fertile ground matured into mighty oaks. The Upjohn Pill and Granule Company (later the Upjohn Company), formed in 1885 in a basement of a building on South Burdick Street, grew into a major supplier of vitamins, penicillin and, thanks to its cadre of researchers, a host of pharmaceutical products. By 1980, it employed 6,400 people. Stryker Corporation, the medical device company founded in 1941 by Homer Stryker, a Kalamazoo surgeon who invented and marketed some of the nation's first orthopedic devices, notched sales of $6 billion in 2007 and employs over 15,000 worldwide. Since their establishment, these two publicly held Fortune 500 members have provided a solid base of employment for Kalamazoo and backed local cultural, economic and philanthropic efforts.

You cannot plan the future by the past.

— EDMUND BURKE

But in the 1950s, although the Kalamazoo economy was still booming, the tide began to slowly turn. The paper industry followed cheaper energy and labor south, with most large companies pulling out of the area. Soon the area's 100-year-old legacy in manufacturing began to lose its base. In 1984, Gibson Guitars' production and headquarters shifted from Kalamazoo to Nashville, Tennessee. In 1982, the last Checker taxicab rolled off the assembly line. (Since then, Checker Motors has reinvented itself as a niche stamper for the automotive industry). In 1999, General Motors closed the massive, 2-million-square-foot Fisher Body plant located on the outskirts of the city. One by one, other icons of the local economy began to disappear, like the Jacobson's and Gilmore's department stores, which had anchored the downtown shopping district and were now replaced by the establishment of large shopping malls in outlying areas. By the late 1990s, in a tale familiar to many cities in the Northeast and Midwest, the faith in the next big thing seemed to be eroding.

The most disconcerting developments surrounded the Upjohn Company, long the largest employer in the region. In 1995, Upjohn merged with the Swedish pharmaceutical company Pharmacia. The headquarters of the combined company was subsequently moved to New Jersey. In 2002, Pharmacia was in turn acquired by Pfizer. The twin mergers resulted in job losses of 4,000 professional, administrative and research positions.

The setbacks could not have come at a more inopportune time. For at the turn of the 21st century, the long-running national economic expansion was losing steam. Meanwhile, Michigan's auto-dependent economy, one of the last to emerge from recession in the early 1990s, continued to feel the effects of the shifting dynamics of the auto industry. As the 20th century glided into the 21st century, Kalamazoo was a community losing confidence, jobs and even population. While the suburban areas had grown rapidly, the city itself had lost residents, from 82,089 in 1960 to 77,000 in 2003. The number of children in the public school system was in a symbiotic decline as well.

The area also had difficulty using its post-secondary academic institutions to bolster the population and talent pipeline. Each year, thousands of college students came to Kalamazoo, which had long been blessed with an extensive system of higher education: Western Michigan University, which evolved from a teacher's college into a level one research institution; Kalamazoo College, an internationally recognized liberal arts college that traces its origins to the 1840s; and Kalamazoo Valley Community College, long recognized as one of the finest institutions of its kind in the nation. But while the community boasts an estimated 44,000 college students, each year upon graduation, most were leaving to seek opportunities elsewhere.

Nothing matters more than the ownership of a vision.

— BILL HYBELS

The challenges Kalamazoo faced were neither unprecedented nor particularly unique. After all, the forces inflicting damage on the region's economy were national — even global — in nature. First, the United States was shifting from a manufacturing economy to a service economy. And the remaining manufacturing firms were physically moving from perceived high-cost regions to low-cost regions. Population growing in the Sunbelt and declining in the so-called Rust Belt, combined with cross-border mergers and globalization, gave rise to a worrisome dichotomy. Companies, business models and entire industries now rise and fall with astonishing speed. Companies routinely merge, acquire competitors, restructure, relocate, expand or fail. Competitors can materialize next door, or on the other side of the world. The creative destruction that characterizes the economy has gone global.

As Kalamazoo moved into the 21st century, the changes occurring there posed a particular dilemma to those concerned with economic development. For in the face of these events, the economic development strategies relied upon in the previous decade suddenly seemed somewhat dated. In the 1990s, it had become common for communities to cobble together large incentive packages to attract manufacturing plants or call centers. But the gains realized by these costly efforts – communities would offer cheap power, free roads, training grants and tax breaks – could be ephemeral; a factory lured by tax breaks could set up shop and then move a few years later, or get shut down when its parent company was acquired. Another avenue followed by some communities was to try and stimulate or actively reinvent an economy by latching on to hot new trends – thus we saw the birth of the "dot-com havens," "cool cities" and "creative communities." But none of these economic theories seemed to hold the answer for Kalamazoo.

While the challenges that Kalamazoo faced may have not been unusual, the community's response was anything but. For rather than throw up their hands, or look to the state or federal government for help, Kalamazoo responded by attacking the problem from a fundamentally different angle. The chosen path has been not so much to attract huge new businesses, but to create an environment where existing and new businesses can grow and thrive. For example, rather than engage in rearguard efforts to retain Pfizer jobs as they are moved elsewhere, the community has tried to figure out ways to enable and encourage former Pfizer scientists to start life science companies. Efforts have centered less on marketing the city, or region, as something it could be, and more on making the most of existing resources. Additionally, the focus has been less on incentives tailored to individual companies, and more on creating infrastructure – the hardware and software – that entrepreneurs and corporations can use as a platform for growth. In Kalamazoo, it is called Community Capitalism.

Community Capitalism can be defined as the focus of key resources on wealth and job creation through the conscious investment in businesses that will in turn grow both community and companies. As practiced in Kalamazoo, it's an economic development strategy that rests on a set of initiatives, partnerships and public-private efforts to revitalize the local economy by tapping into existing resources. Rather than a centrally planned group of policies, the efforts have grown up organically, taken shape and coherence and fed upon one another. The actors involved are varied: families and individuals, for-profit companies and universities, hospitals and public-private partnerships, large Fortune 500 corporations and two-person start-ups, service and manufacturing industries and the public school system and community foundations.

Most new jobs won't come from our biggest employers.
They will come from our smallest.
We've got to do everything we can to make
entrepreneurial dreams a reality.

— ROSS PEROT

These initiatives, which focus on different areas, are led by different individuals and groups – although the umbrella organization Southwest Michigan First has played a critical role in the overall strategy. And yet they all share something in common. Each represents an effort to shape the local economic environment so that it can simultaneously weather the changes wrought by the larger global economic environment and afford local residents the ability to realize the new opportunities the world now presents. Small communities like Kalamazoo can't stop or even divert the big macroeconomic forces that are altering the economy. But they can create new infrastructure and help shape the local environment. They can help highlight and emphasize the components of the local economy that can, in turn, attract human and financial capital.

In many ways, Kalamazoo is a unique community, with unique resources. We believe, however, that the components of Kalamazoo's strategy can be replicated elsewhere; and many of them already have, although they look different. It is our belief that through the examples offered by Kalamazoo and the stories from around the world, you will discover that the principles of Community Capitalism can indeed be replicated globally. More importantly, you will witness that with the proper mindset, approach, sense of partnership and innovative thinking, successful change is indeed possible and that you can indeed re-imagine the economic potential of your community.

CHAPTER I

PLACE:
ROCKS, MARBLES AND SAND

Live out of your imagination, not your history.

— STEPHEN COVEY

Perhaps the best way to think about a place is to use the popular thought experiment once used by a professor in a college course. He set a big glass bowl on a desk and filled it with large rocks. He then asked his students if the bowl was full. When they answered "yes," he poured in a bag of marbles. He again asked if it was full. When the students again responded in the affirmative, he took a bag of sand and poured it in.

Sure, you've heard that one before. But now let's use it as a metaphor for a place. In order for a city to attract businesses and retail shops to its streets, keep residents within its borders and offer a venue for culture and entertainment, it needs some rocks, a few more marbles and a bunch of sand.

Let's start with an easy example. New York City. Lots of rocks there. The Empire State Building. Rockefeller Center. Yankee Stadium. Central Park. For marbles, we can count Radio City Music Hall, the Metropolitan Museum of Art, the Statue of Liberty, LaGuardia Airport, Grand Central Station and Macy's department store. And sand, well it's everywhere in New York City – Tavern on the Green, Tiffany's, FAO Schwartz, Serendipity 3 and Zabar's.

Now let's consider the typical "old economy" town. Many of these manufacturing towns across the Midwest and Mid-Atlantic regions of the United States have seen better days due to the manufacturing industry's decline. Factories have been abandoned, railroad stations left in disrepair, brick buildings allowed to crumble, paint on store fronts chipped, apartment buildings deserted, small businesses relocated and residents gone to the suburbs. What are these towns to do for their rocks, marbles and sand?

Now let's consider Kalamazoo. In 1867, the Kalamazoo Paper Company was built along the Kalamazoo River and many other huge paper mills followed its lead. At the turn of the century, the Kalamazoo Corset Company employed over 800 women and was the largest corset factory in the world. In 1917, Orville Gibson established his Gibson-Mandolin-Guitar Manufacturing Company at its location on Parsons Street, where it meticulously crafted instruments for seven decades. The Kalamazoo Stove Company, with its motto "A Kalamazoo Direct to You," Checker Motors Company, with its famed yellow-checkered cabs, and the Kalamazoo Sled Company, once the world's largest manufacturer of children's sleds, all had their birth in Kalamazoo. Not many other towns in America can boast so many innovative and historically relevant institutions. And with these institutions, came the usual government buildings, quaint churches, stately homes and community parks. Kalamazoo was even once seen as a pioneer of downtown redevelopment, building the nation's first downtown pedestrian mall in 1959 by blocking off traffic from three blocks on Burdick Street. But enough history. Let's get back to the lesson at hand.

By the late 1990s, downtown Kalamazoo faced the same challenges as many other American "old economy" downtowns, large and small. Suburban development, big box retailers, the decline of department stores and the disappearance of some large employers had led to an exodus of workers, residents and businesses. The past 20 years had seen

Kalamazoo's downtown workforce go from 26,000 to a low of about 11,000. The main culprits were the migration of the paper mills due to excess capacity; workforce reductions at Upjohn, then Pharmacia and later Pfizer; the loss of 700 employees when National City merged with First of America; and department stores like Jacobson's and Gilmore's, longtime anchors of the downtown retail district, closing in 1997 and 1999, respectively. Given the shift of manufacturing to other regions and countries and the resulting decline of its employment base, factories were left abandoned and national retailers were not exactly rushing to get in. With the large rocks being extracted, one by one, from the downtown's bowl, it was increasingly challenging for the marbles and sand – i.e. medium and small businesses – to survive.

But Kalamazoo, with its historic past and tremendous pride, was not about to become a decaying city of the past. To quote the old cliché, "When the going gets tough, the tough get going." And Kalamazoo certainly has proven to be tough. Its response was a combination of individual and institutional efforts, entrepreneurial undertakings and public-private partnerships aimed at bringing new construction, businesses and capital to the downtown area. The most significant developments were two large-scale exercises in Community Capitalism – the Radisson Plaza Hotel and Bronson Methodist Hospital – which have become rocks. Both ventures began with financial returns as a secondary objective. But due to their focus on excellence and performance, they have provided excellent returns – financial *and* civic – and inspired other development efforts.

It's impossible for a city to be a world-class business community without a business class hotel. And in Kalamazoo, the Radisson Plaza Hotel at Kalamazoo Center serves that function. On a typical day, it's a hive of activity. Daily events might range from a breakfast sponsored by one of the area's health insurers to discuss wellness in the workplace, the hotel florist busily preparing centerpieces for a wedding, a business lunch at one of the hotel's four restaurants, group meetings simultaneously occurring in one of the 22 conference and banquet rooms, employees of nearby companies stopping in for coffee at the hotel coffee and news shop, a group of visitors perusing the one-of-a-kind designer clothing and accessories at Sydney's, a couple listening to a pianist on the grand piano or an evening fundraiser in the ballroom. That is not to mention its numerous guests coming and going through the lobby.

The Radisson, now one of the top performers in the large multinational chain, has undergone a renaissance in the last decade and has come to be the visual rock in the center of downtown Kalamazoo. But the path to its success was hard-traveled. Built in the 1970s as a public-private partnership between Inland Steel and the city of Kalamazoo and originally flagged as a Hilton, it failed and then went through a series of owners. In the early 1990s, the Upjohn Company bought the property, invested $22 million in a renovation and used it primarily as a facility for sales training. After its merger with Pharmacia however, the company announced it was going to divest all non-pharmaceutical businesses. That meant Kalamazoo faced the prospect of having an empty 650,000-square-foot facility in the middle of a struggling city.

Enter Kalamazoo entrepreneur Bill Johnston. "Several people in the community came to me and said, 'You are the obvious next owner of this property,'" said Bill Johnston, Chairman of the Greenleaf Companies, as well as Chairman of Southwest Michigan First. "I looked around and there wasn't anybody else behind me in line."

> *I looked around and there wasn't*
> *anybody else behind me in line.*
>
> **— BILL JOHNSTON**

In May 2000, the Catalyst Development Company, an entity formed by Bill Johnston and a unit of the Greenleaf Companies, took ownership of the hotel. "Initially my interest in the property was a benevolent interest," he said. But Bill Johnston wanted to make it work also as a business and set about transforming the property's structure and staff. A multimillion-dollar, five-year renovation added a tower and 76 suites, bringing the hotel's total space to 850,000 square feet. The twin towers that now adorn the exterior serve as a downtown hallmark.

The internal offerings were upgraded as well. Today, the complex boasts 341 rooms, sufficient meeting space to make it the fourth-largest conference and convention property in Michigan, a full-service spa, the Kalamazoo Athletic Club, four distinct restaurants, a florist, elegant shopping and even a 5,000-gallon saltwater aquarium.

Most notably, the hotel's four unique restaurant offerings have become some pretty important sand. Zazio's offers a modern Italian dining experience complete with an interactive chef's table. Webster's, with its copper and brass display kitchen, is a four-star fine dining affair. Old Burdick's Bar & Grill has become a local and popular haunt featuring round-the-clock sporting events on a television-video wall containing nine high-definition screens. And finally, SOL World Café, lives up to its "sunny" name with its brightly lit breakfast and lunch buffet room.

The hotel, complemented by its restaurants and propelled by the Radisson's talent-driven workforce, has earned itself a four-diamond distinction. In addition, said Bill Johnston, "Of all the Radissons in this country, we are rated number one in terms of customer satisfaction." The Radisson has helped to greatly rejuvenate the downtown's nightlife. Once the lights go down in Kalamazoo, people hop from restaurant to restaurant, restaurant to event or restaurant to venue, both inside and out of the complex – to the tune of almost one million pairs of feet coming through the property yearly.

A little over a half-mile south of the Radisson, another community-minded infrastructure project has served a similar function of injecting the downtown full of people. Since its founding in 1900, Bronson Methodist Hospital, a locally owned, not-for-profit hospital, had grown into a major medical institution and, by the late 1990s, had outgrown its current physical infrastructure while becoming the

1961. GORONGOSA PARK, MOZAMBIQUE, AFRICA. Movie stars, celebrities and tourists arrived by the busload to view the wildebeest, zebra, elephants, buffalo and waterbuck that traversed the well-watered terrain in some of the densest herds on the continent. The only violence was natural; lionesses roamed freely, driving quarry grazing alongside woodland edges into ambushes in order to feed their pride.

THE PARK IS OPEN FOR VISITORS

1974. LISBON, PORTUGAL. A bloodless, socialist-inspired military coup known as the Carnation Revolution overthrew the dictatorship and installed a modern democracy. The new regime granted independence to its remaining colonies in Africa. Mozambique became independent on June 25, 1975.

1977. GORONGOSA PARK, MOZAMBIQUE, AFRICA. A civil war erupted. Anti-government forces hunkered down outside Gorongosa in order to use its shelter and abundant food resources. The park became a battlefield. The violence was man-made; land mines were detonated, shots rang out uncontrolled and animals were slaughtered.

1986. BOSTON, MASSACHUSETTS. A student at Harvard's Kennedy School of Government, Greg Carr and Scott Jones, a lab scientist from the Massachusetts Institute of Technology, started Boston Technology, a start-up company providing voice-mail services to telephone companies formed as a result of the AT&T breakup. Within four years, Boston Technology was the number one voice-mail provider to telecommunications companies.

1992. GORONGOSA PARK, MOZAMBIQUE AFRICA. The Rome General Peace Accords ended the civil war. A United Nations' peace-keeping force returned peace to the land. A new constitution established a multi-party government and market-based economy. People returned to their villages. Those whose homes had been destroyed moved into the park and cleared the land for farming. Wild animals were harvested for sustenance.

1999. CAMBRIDGE, MASSACHUSETTS. After serving as chair of Boston Technology until 1998 and of Prodigy Internet Corporation from 1996 to 1998, Greg Carr, now worth over $200 million, resigned from all of his profitable posts and founded the Carr Foundation. The Carr Foundation, a non-profit organization, was dedicated to the environment, human rights and the arts. Through the foundation, Greg Carr purchased a defunct Aryan Nations property and donated it to North Idaho College for a peace park, began the Market Theater in Harvard Square, founded the Museum of Idaho and Boise's Anne Frank

Human Rights Memorial, started a radio station in Afghanistan and gave $18 million to Harvard for the establishment of the Carr Center for Human Rights Policy.

2004. GORONGOSA PARK, MOZAMBIQUE, AFRICA. The main camp in the park at Chitengo was in ruins. No busloads of movie stars, celebrities or tourists arrived at all. The great animal herds had been decimated – the herd of buffalo once numbered at 14,000 was at 50. Greg Carr made a return trip to Mozambique in search of a destination for a vacation development. In 2000, Greg Carr had been impressed by Carlos dos Santos, the Mozambican ambassador to the United Nations. The ambassador's story of one of the poorest nations on earth with its per capita income of $310, average life expectancy of 40, rampant HIV epidemic and undeveloped infrastructure made Greg Carr want to do something for the country. The Gorongosa landscape made an indelible impression on him as he flew over the area. In October, Greg Carr signed a deal with Mozambique's Ministry of Tourism promising $500,000 for the restoration of the park.

2005. GORONGOSA PARK, MOZAMBIQUE, AFRICA. In November, Greg Carr signed a new agreement with the park. He pledged $40 million over 30 years for protection and renewal of the park and to ensure the welfare of the communities around it. His plan called for everything from ecological restoration to economic development. That year 1,000 visitors came to the park.

2006. GORONGOSA PARK, MOZAMBIQUE, AFRICA. Renovations on the Chitengo camp began. The first herd of buffalo was introduced. Reforestation on the mountain was begun. Community improvement programs were initiated and the park staff grew from 100 to 500. The park was visited by 5,000 people this year. Greg Carr began spending every other month at Gorongosa focusing on community relations and the concept of eco-tourism, which is the promotion of travel to natural areas that conserve the environment and improve the well-being of local people.

2007. GORONGOSA PARK, MOZAMBIQUE AFRICA. About 800 animals of different species were introduced into the park. The park was open for visitors thanks to the efforts of Greg Carr.

largest employer in downtown Kalamazoo. But Bronson had even greater ambitions.

"We've always tried to be out in front of trends," said Frank Sardone, Chief Executive Officer of Bronson Healthcare Group. "We had the concept over a decade ago that we could transform the way health care is conducted, and that required a new way of thinking about how we deliver health care." This requirement would involve a significant investment in their "four walls" which were actually a warren of buildings, some of which dated back to 1905.

When the hospital's board of directors, composed of local citizens, confronted the decision in 1992 over whether to stay downtown or move to a suburban location, they fully considered the challenges facing Kalamazoo and decided to stay and be part of the solution. As one of the city's oldest corporate citizens, Bronson had seen the city move through several transitions. "Our downtown was reinventing itself for the third and fourth time to be something that our economy and city needed," said Bob Doud, Vice President of Public Affairs at Bronson. And so Bronson embarked upon an eight-year, $210 million project to replace its clinical capabilities with a new facility, built on a 14-acre site adjacent to the century-old hospital campus.

If you really want to succeed,
you must outwork your adversary.

— JOSEPH JAWORSKI

Today, Bronson Hospital, with about 4,100 employees, including a medical staff of 700, is the largest employer in the city. It has 380 light-filled private rooms, a Level 1 Trauma Center, the region's only accredited Chest Pain Center and is one of four children's hospitals in the state. The new facility has brought all sorts of economic benefits, beyond the jobs created during construction. The hospital's reputation has grown as a quality health care center, becoming a magnet to downtown, for patients and their visitors. "Our patient volume has grown by over 43 percent since 2000," said Frank Sardone, "and over 40 percent of our patients come from outside Kalamazoo." Building the new facility has also resulted in more physicians having offices on the campus. And the hospital encourages its staff, employees, patients and their family members to take advantage of its downtown location.

As one of the large rocks filling in Kalamazoo's downtown, Bronson has also made efforts to encourage the introduction of marbles and sand. It has taken steps to involve itself in the community's revival by encouraging the use of existing resources. For example, when the new hospital opened, Bronson helped the city convert a former outpatient facility into a new criminal justice facility. Bronson, with the aid of other downtown residents, chipped in to improve city streets. It also started a program that has provided no-interest loans to employees who want to buy homes in adjacent neighborhoods.

And it is said that no downtown is complete without the physical presence of an academic institution of higher learning. Toward that end, a second campus of Kalamazoo Valley Community College was established in downtown Kalamazoo in 1994. The 58,000-square-foot Arcadia Commons Campus was part of a community/business/education partnership responsible for the renovation and revitalization of a significant portion of the historic downtown area. The Arcadia campus provides customized training for business and industry, a wide range of non-credit seminars and workshops and coordinated off-campus services.

In 2004, the 48,000-square-foot Center for New Media was opened as an additional part of the Arcadia Commons Campus to teach the creativity and skills needed by employees in the Information Age in order to better prepare them for a world market dependent on the Internet and e-commerce. Programs include graphic design, video game art, animation, e-business and others. In addition, in May of each odd-numbered year, Kalamazoo Valley Community College hosts the Kalamazoo Animation Festival International in downtown Kalamazoo.

Independent and student animators from around the world take part in the prestigious competition, which offers both notoriety and cash prizes to pioneering animators.

Understanding the demographics of your community is important, but understanding the culture of your community is even more important.

— RICK WARREN

When the city's downtown museum, the Kalamazoo Valley Museum, founded in 1881, looked to expand in 1996, the Kalamazoo Valley Community College Foundation largely participated in the private and public $20 million fund-raising effort to create a new 60,000-square-foot state-of-the-art museum structure, designed by the renowned architect E. Verner Johnson. The money helped the museum to continue in its mission to "preserve and interpret the heritage of southwest Michigan and provide life-long learning opportunities to engage children and adults in history, science and technology." Residents and schools alike benefit from its year-round exhibits revealing worldly secrets on everything from weather patterns to Egyptian mummies and its resources which include a domed planetarium.

The above mentioned efforts echo other initiatives to create marbles and sand, including those backed by the Kalamazoo Community Foundation, a longtime champion of downtown Kalamazoo. When the city's historic outdoor pedestrian walking mall needed serious updating in 2000, the foundation was there with funding to refurbish the brick street and revamp it with limited parking. This was done as part of a successful effort to encourage patronage at shops and restaurants along the walkway.

The Kalamazoo Community Foundation also led the effort when the city wanted to create an outdoor gathering place for festivals and other special events. Completed in May 2004, the $2.25 million

Arcadia Creek Festival Place offers a band shell with a permanent stage, a jumping fountain plaza, children's play area, covered picnic and special event area, landscape art and gorgeous theme gardens filled with bedding plants from the nation's "Bedding Plant Capital." (And yes, Kalamazoo is the leading producer of bedding plants in the United States). The site is home to numerous community events including the Blues Fest, Rib Fest and the Taste of Kalamazoo, which draw over 150,000 visitors to downtown Kalamazoo annually.

"Downtown Kalamazoo is the heart of the county, and if it is solid and pumping strongly, it will feed blood to the extremities," said Jack Hopkins, Chief Executive Officer of the Kalamazoo Community Foundation. The Foundation has also offered loan guarantees to redevelop warehouses into loft apartments and condos with exposed brick walls, cathedral ceilings, hardwood floors and ample natural light. For example, it lent $784,000 at 1.5 percent interest to Downtown Tomorrow, Inc., a non-profit real estate development group, to buy a building that formerly housed Koopsen's paint store on the north Kalamazoo Mall. Downtown Tomorrow, Inc. then worked with developers to build 20 condominiums on the site above a hospice care center servicing southwest Michigan that rival those in other larger metropolitan areas.

*Downtown Kalamazoo is the heart
of the county, and if it is solid and pumping strongly,
it will feed blood to the extremities.*

— JACK HOPKINS

Private entrepreneurs have also contributed to the downtown's vitality. Ken Miller, a Western Michigan University alumnus and corporate financier, became interested in restaurants as a hobby and has developed his "hobby" into much more. Over the years, he has built up Millennium Restaurant Group, a five-restaurant operation, two of which are in downtown Kalamazoo.

Nostalgia. Longing for the past. Craving that special feeling that one feels when thinking of the quintessential American town and neighborhood of long ago. When streets were neat and clean. When building facades were pristine. When people walked to work or the local shop. When people waved hello and stopped to chat. When children ran carefree from neighborhood house to house.

In today's city planning, such an approach to designing cities, towns and neighborhoods is called "New Urbanism." A New Urbanist neighborhood resembles an old European village – homes and business are clustered together, schools are centrally located so that kids can walk to and from them and recreational areas are arranged to foster a sense of community. Designers of such towns focus on green architecture, historic preservation and accessibility.

WHAT'S OLD IS NEW AGAIN

In Osceola County, Florida, in a little community called Celebration, one can find such a place. Originally planned by The Walt Disney Company (which has since divested most of its control over the town since its foundation), this unincorporated master-planned community was home to 9,500 residents in 3,745 households as of 2004. Built in the early 1990s by the Celebration Company which was formed by the Disney Development Company, the community encompasses approximately 4,900 acres of land and was the result of $2.5 billion of investment.

It is "legend" that Celebration was created based upon Walt Disney's original concept for Epcot. While it is true that it lies on land that used to be part of Walt Disney World Resort, it bears no resemblance to Walt Disney's dream of a place where there would be no home ownership, no unemployment, no traffic as a result of underground roads and a climate controlled by a dome. Rather than turning out as a futuristic society, the community is a modern version of an ideal town of yesteryear.

The community of Celebration is broken down into several villages or neighborhoods, each with its own character. Residents choose which village is right for them based upon their own or their family's likes. Residences – homes, townhomes, condominiums, apartments, etc. – are available near the downtown area, the golf course, gardens, pools, highways, parks or exclusive facilities, and in secluded spots, quiet places, wooded areas or active neighborhoods.

The community is governed by a set of rules and covenants similar to other planned communities. While it is rumored that they are eerily stringent (*White curtains only!*), this is not the case. Rather, they are

aimed at maintaining property values by encouraging home maintenance and upkeep. And who can really argue with these: only two cars
per home can be parked on the street, trash cans can only be visible
on pick-up day and campers can only be left curbside for so long.
Let's face it... who really likes to drive around that boat trailer left on
the side of the road next door more than once? So while it is true that
one of the streets in the community may be named Wisteria Lane, the
neighborhood association is nothing like the one seen on the ABC
network on Sunday evenings.

Living in the community has many benefits. Community pools, parks
and walking trails are scattered throughout. The downtown area is
modeled after an idealized picture perfect small 1930s American
town. Centered around Market Street, the downtown is home to the
town hall, post office, grocery store, retail stores, restaurants, offices
and a movie theater. Around the lake, more shops and fine restaurants dot the landscape to provide ample entertainment opportunities. A 60-bed hospital and emergency room is on call for residents.
The 18-hole public golf course was designed by Robert Trent Jones,
Sr. and Robert Trent Jones, Jr. The community also has its own
public elementary, middle and high schools. The area benefits from
an extremely low crime rate and easy access to highways and thor-
oughfares.

In addition, community events foster exactly what they are meant to
do – bring the community together. They include a Fourth of July
celebration, the "Great American Pie Festival," an exotic car show, a
"Posh Pooch" festival and, in a place that pretty much offers summer
year-round, falling "leaves" in October and "snowfall" (or, shall we say,
soap bubbles) in the month of December. But beyond that, it's the
overall atmosphere of the place that brings everyone out of their front
doors to mix, mingle and play.

So while Celebration, Florida is fabled to be either Walt Disney's vision
of Epcot or the real Wisteria Lane, it is really only one thing – a great
place to live.

In the late 1990s, Ken Miller sensed opportunity in the down-town's shuttered department stores along the Kalamazoo Mall. In 1998, he opened the Epic Bistro, designated a "haven for the wine and food lover," in the former Jacobson's building. "National chains weren't going to come downtown," said Ken Miller, who also chairs Downtown Tomorrow, Inc. "If something was going to happen, it would have to be local people doing it." And again in 2000, when real estate developer Josh Weiner turned the former site of the other defunct department store, Gilmore's, into a three-building complex anchored by the Epic Center, a cultural arts center, Ken Miller saw opportunity. To fill the ground-level space, he decided to take a chance and create his dream – a jazz club. The Union, his dream turned reality, sought help from an important community resource – Western Michigan University. A trustee at the university, Ken Miller worked out an arrangement with Western Michigan University's prestigious jazz program for the university to provide performers 26 weeks per year at $500 per night per gig to the Union. While the club has hired booking agents to fill the remainder of the slots, "It has wound up that Western Michigan University has people in here 45 weeks per year," said Ken Miller.

*If something was going to happen,
it would have to be local people doing it.*

– KEN MILLER

Kalamazoo has been conscientious to care for all its citizens. When Meijer, the Midwest super-store giant, pulled out of the lower income north side of the city, that neighborhood was left without an easily accessible grocery store. The city of Kalamazoo and the Northside Economic Potential Group teamed up with Southwest Michigan First, the state of Michigan and the Kalamazoo Community Foundation to bring Felpausch Grocery Store to the area. Working with the city of

Kalamazoo to create a Renaissance Zone, the new store not only provided the residents with a place to shop and call their own, but also enhanced the neighborhood's economic status.

All these efforts have created a community of like-minded, interested leaders intent on restoring economic vitality to downtown Kalamazoo – working in harmony, instead of in competition, as one might think when it comes to making money. And there are plans afoot for more big rocks – and many more marbles. Downtown organizations, which include the Downtown Development Authority, Downtown Tomorrow, Inc. and Downtown Kalamazoo, Inc., continue to work together to identify possible projects. One possible project is the concept of an arena for Kalamazoo's minor league hockey team and for Western Michigan University's basketball and hockey teams. Land has been assembled, which includes a parcel donated to Western Michigan University by the owner of an abandoned auto dealership a few blocks from the Radisson, in downtown Kalamazoo that could be a site for such an undertaking. And other investors, including local entrepreneurs and the Kalamazoo Community Foundation, have come up with funds to help amass additional nearby land. Altogether, this group controls a nine-acre, four-city-block site where an arena could be built.

Kalamazoo never rests on its laurels, because it knows that transformation and revival are never complete. The Community Capitalism efforts to revive downtown Kalamazoo have produced results. And all the activity has piqued the interest of out-of-town investors as well. In November 2006, Rave Motion Pictures, a Texas-based company, opened a 70,000-square-foot, 14-screen movie complex with stadium seating in the heart of downtown. The complex acts as yet another magnet, drawing thousands of people downtown on evenings and weekends.

Looking out the window from the upper floors of the Radisson, one can see the new Miller Canfield Building rising nearby, at the corner of Rose and South Streets. Ground was broken on the 60,000-square-foot, Class A+ office building in September 2006. Adjacent to Bronson Park, the luxury space offers views of neighboring churches,

Boise, Idaho. What comes to mind? To most of us, potatoes. And in Boise, they like them big and small – really, really small. Small as in microchips.

Apparently, Boise is where it's at these days if you are into technology. And surprisingly, most of us have no idea where it's at – Boise that is. Well get ready to get acquainted.

HOME TO ALL THE RIGHT KINDS OF "CHIPS"

Listed in the Top 10 lists of the "Hottest Tech Cities" and "Best Places" for business and careers by periodicals such as *Newsweek*, *Forbes* and *Inc.*, Boise is home to Micron, one of the world's leading providers of advanced semiconductor solutions and memory storage, and Hewlett-Packard, which started its laser printer business there. Boise ranks as the city with the second-highest technology GDP growth in the United States according to the Milken Institute and, in September 2007, *USA Today* pointed out that Boise is the "heart of America's biggest economic boom" in the "state with the nation's fastest-growing economy." With 72 percent of all of Idaho's exports coming from the technology sector (not the spud sector), Boise boasts the number one payroll in the state and an astonishing unemployment rate of a little over 2 percent.

With Micron and Hewlett-Packard both anchoring and developing talent, Boise has seen its share of small- and medium-sized company start-ups. Also, companies routinely move and expand there. Take Treetop Tech, for example. Founded in 1997 in Boise, the company could have easily centered in India or Silicon Valley. But the full-service customer software development and professional staffing firm was drawn to Boise's lower housing and labor costs, regulatory environment and lower taxes – which offer companies like Treetop Tech a competitive place to operate in a globalized economy and still keep costs low and quality high.

What draws companies to Boise? Maybe it's because of the talent developed there, maybe it's because of the nurturing business environment, maybe it's because Idaho ranks as the 13th lowest state in the cost of doing business or maybe it's because 42 percent of Boise's 567,000 residents have college degrees, according to a May 2007 CNBC "On the Money" report. Not only is the technology sector doing well, but other industries are blossoming too – employment is up 650 percent since 2000 in the online publishing and broadcasting industries, with the wireless telecom and financial services industries also providing plenty of opportunities.

Beyond all that, what is it that attracts people to a city seemingly in the middle of nowhere? Maybe it's the love of place and loyalty that Boise instills in its residents. Surrounded by the Owyhee Mountains in a space where the desert plateau meets the base of the Rocky Mountains, Boise combines a feeling of the Old West with Silicon Valley. Even neighborhoods show this dichotomy offering everything from frontier-like living to cosmopolitan lofts. And those neighborhoods offer residents a stable housing market, home appreciation and one of the nation's hot spots for real estate investment opportunities.

Boise has it all – desert, rivers, mountains and lakes. Residents and visitors enjoy rafting on the Payette River, mountain biking in the foothills, skiing at the Bogus Basin Ski Resort and abundant hunting and fishing along the Snake River. Its standard of living is nationally recognized too. *Forbes* and *Money* magazines rank Boise as one of the top 10 places to live because of its access to recreational activities, employment opportunities and the lifestyle it affords. In 2006, *National Geographic* put its "spotlight" on Boise in its list of the top 31 adventure towns.

Boise is also Idaho's state capital (thus offering numerous employment opportunities in government). What else would attract people to live in a downtown, where its Main Street runs parallel to the Boise River? Maybe it's its one-of-a-kind blue football field. Credited for propelling the Boise State University Broncos to national prominence, the blue synthetic grass provides lots of problems for the opponents of the home "blue and orange" team.

Forgotten about potatoes by now? Well don't. Boise is home to one of the world's largest potato processors, the J. R. Simplot Company. The company annually turns out 3 billion pounds of French fries and other potato products worldwide; that 3 billion number matches the company's annual sales of about $3 billion, which result from its combined agri-businesses – food, fertilizer, turf, horticultural and cattle feed.

And think potato chips have nothing to do with microchips? Think again. Here's a little secret ... Micron was started by a group of entrepreneurs in the basement of a building owned by Mr. J. R. Simplot. And when Micron needed a little extra cash to get going, Simplot himself contributed additional funding. So you can create microchips from potato chips after all.

People love living in Boise. So remember if you're ever asked, "What's cookin' in Boise?," you can answer, "Apparently, just about everything!"

civic structures, artistic fountains, historic sculptures and the park's extraordinary setting that hosts summer concerts, art exhibits, holiday festivals and year-round picture perfect views of the changing seasons. The building is named for its anchor tenant, the law firm Miller Canfield, whose 70 attorneys and staffers will occupy the top two floors. Developed by the Catalyst Development Company and opened in January 2008, this is the first major office building constructed in downtown Kalamazoo in more than 20 years.

> *Greatness is not a function of circumstance.*
> *Greatness as it turns out is largely a matter of*
> *conscious choice and discipline.*
>
> — JIM COLLINS

Taken together, these efforts to create a world-class hotel, a hospital with a national reputation, urbane restaurants, state-of-the-art entertainment options and high-end office space, stand as highly visible messages that downtown Kalamazoo has a promising future. But they are far more than symbolic efforts, far more than rocks, marbles and sand. They represent tangible generators of economic growth, important sources of employment, and people pumps – entities that attract large numbers of people to the area and, in turn, encourage them to patronize other businesses in the area. While they rely on using and leveraging the community's existing resources, they also result in the creation of important new infrastructure that enriches life in downtown Kalamazoo – and in the entire region.

And for those of you who were not really sure…Yes, Kalamazoo is really a place!

CHAPTER 2

CAPITAL:
SHOW ME THE MONEY

To keep a lamp burning,
we have to keep putting oil in it.

— MOTHER TERESA

"Show me the money." It's not just the most remembered line from the 1996 film *Jerry Maguire*; it's the mantra of our economy. In theory and in practice, capital flows anywhere in the globe where opportunities can be found.

Capital can also be quite parochial and provincial. That can be a daunting obstacle to overcome for a community like Kalamazoo in 2003 faced with a major company downsizing its workforce and eager to do something about it.

Kalamazoo's response was unique.

Rather than succumb to self-pity, it focused on the simple reality of the situation: Pfizer was downsizing its workforce in Kalamazoo and relocating it to other parts of the world; Kalamazoo wanted Pfizer scientists to "stick around" and start companies of their own; Kalamazoo needed capital to encourage and be able to finance this effort; Kalamazoo did not have a large pool of available capital; and capital existed around the country, but capital residing in life science and technology funds tended to focus on existing clusters close to its home on the coasts.

In response, Kalamazoo inverted the challenge posed by this last point. Most communities would have gone out and tried to lure out-of-town capital. But Kalamazoo understood that would have been like banging its head against the wall. The life science industry had historically and indigenously clustered itself geographically for perfectly natural reasons: the proximity to exceptional institutions of higher learning and renowned hospitals, the natural concentration of venture capital, a strong physical and information infrastructure, specialized talent and training, industry-leading companies in such technology sectors as semiconductors and networking, government policies that encourage business development and the physical location of established industry giants in those areas. Examples of such life science clusters are San Francisco, California; Minneapolis, Minnesota; Boston, Massachusetts; and Warsaw, Indiana. Kalamazoo understood that the capital available in those areas would not find its way there.

Life science is a particularly capital-intensive industry. Start-ups require substantial funds to conduct basic research and then take discoveries through trials to the point where they can be viable products. Kalamazoo is not lacking for wealth – it is home to large philanthropic foundations, Fortune 500 corporations, asset management and advisory businesses and plenty of wealthy individuals. But unlike other hotbeds of life science development, Kalamazoo had not developed a venture capital community – the network of investors, bankers, analysts and other professionals who could provide the cash, expertise and connections to capital markets and corporations. "If you ranked states on the basis of patent discovery, Michigan ranked in the top tier. But if you ranked states on capital formation, Michigan ranked last," said Bill Johnston.

So, if you couldn't get capital to come to you, what would you do, if you were Kalamazoo? Give up? No. Get frustrated? No. Say, "Oh well, there is nothing you can do?" No.

Leaders in Kalamazoo knew they were largely powerless to change the state's geographical position in relation to existing venture capital. But they could do something about the region's own lack of venture capital. Again, Kalamazoo honed in on the fact that capital *focuses on existing clusters close to its home.* Then, the community decided to do the unthinkable. If it was already creating the infrastructure for business creation in places such as the soon-to-be-discussed Southwest Michigan Innovation Center and Midlink Business Park, then it could certainly create the capital that it needed. And that's what Kalamazoo did – to the tune of $50 million.

Kalamazoo's solution was to create homegrown venture capital that could attract businesses to the area and partner with other sources of capital. Its strategy was to form a venture capital fund with a unique set of mandates, to encourage the growth of other venture capital organizations with a local orientation and build a network of interested investors.

In southwest Michigan, we literally have everything you need to get from discovery to phase one trials to manufacturing to sales.

- PAT MORAND

In 2005, Southwest Michigan First formed the Southwest Michigan First Life Science Fund, a $50 million venture fund to invest in the local life science community. The fund has a dual bottom line. It sought, naturally, to make money for its investors. But its primary goal was to "spur economic development and retain intellectual capital within the Kalamazoo region," according to Pat Morand, Managing Director of the Southwest Michigan First Life Science Fund.

The fund achieves its primary goal by making sure that a company in which it invests is either located in southwest Michigan or does a significant, demonstrable amount of business with southwest Michigan-

REPUBLIC OF GHANA. Located in Western Africa. Borders Côte d'Ivoire to the west, Burkina Faso in the north, Togo to the east and the Gulf of Guinea on the south. Estimated population: around 24,000,000. Females make up 50.2 percent of the population. Home to 3,275-square-mile Lake Volta, the world's largest man-made lake. Total area is 92,098 square miles. Highest elevation is Mount Afadjato, 2,900 feet above sea level. Average temperature is 79°F. Lowest average temperature during the year is 74°F. Average monthly precipitation is 2.46 inches. In 2005, GDP was $53.125 billion. Female literacy rate is 45.7 percent.

BEHIND EVERY GOOD WOMAN IS ... ANOTHER GOOD WOMAN

STATE OF NEW HAMPSHIRE. Located in the Northeastern part of the United States. Bounded by Quebec, Canada to the north, Maine and the Atlantic Ocean to the east, Massachusetts on the south and Vermont to the west. Population is estimated around 1,275,000. Females make up 50.7 percent of the population. Home to Lake Winnipesaukee which covers 72 square miles. Total area is 9,304 square miles. Highest elevation is Mount Washington at 6,288 feet. Average temperature is 46°F. Lowest average temperature during the year is 21°F. Average monthly precipitation is 3.2 inches. In 2005, GSP (state counterpart of GDP) was $55.061 billion. Female literacy rate of the United States is 95.3 percent.

REPUBLIC OF GHANA. Home of aspiring entrepreneur, Comfort Owusu. Business is porridge.

STATE OF NEW HAMPSHIRE. Home of founder of Dakin Partners, Dana Dakin. Business is in packaging institutional investment organizations.

Put it all together: **WOMENSTRUST.**

In 2003, Dana Dakin felt the need to start something new. Her business, Dakin Partners, was so successful that it was *too busy*. She decided that her life could be divided in thirds – "first you learn, then you earn and finally you return." It was now time for the *third* third.

Dana Dakin arrived in the village of Pokuase, near the northern perimeter of Ghana's capital Accra, with the name of her personal trainer's father in her pocket in March 2003. Her intention was to help Pokuase's 10,000 residents, many of whom are at the bottom rung of a nation in which nearly half of the population lives in poverty. During a Sunday church service, Dana Dakin announced her intention to lend money to women interested in starting businesses of their own.

Her version of "microlending" required women to form cohesive groups of four to six in order to apply for a loan. Peer pressure would be the binding force. Each member of the group would receive an individual loan of $22 to $33 and each would be collectively responsible for the entire group's repayment of the loan. The interest rate was 15 percent, payable in four months. (Typical interest rates in Ghana are around 100 percent for shorter time frames.)

WomensTrust, Inc., a Ghanaian non-government organization, was born with the mission of supporting "social and economic empowerment for women and girls living in poverty through microenterprise, education and health care." Dana Dakin initially funded the project with $18,000 made from the sale of her Volvo. Funding later came from hometown friends, business contacts and other interested parties. That first year, loans totaling $2,022 were given to 73 women.

By August 2007, WomensTrust aimed to have 1,000 clients. Today, the loan is $55, payable in four months with a 13 percent interest rate. The program has been extended to offer groups that repay their loans further levels of funding from $60–$220. To date, WomensTrust has loaned over $100,000 with a 90 percent repayment rate. Money obtained from interest is used to cover all administrative costs.

Loans are used by hairdressers, bakers, seamstresses and sellers of household necessities – from cassavas to shoes. Money is used to increase inventory, purchase raw materials in large quantities to reduce transportation costs and expand product offerings.

And the program hasn't stopped there. The Keep-Girls-In-School Program offers scholarships for girls who may have otherwise dropped out of school to remain in attendance. Stipends for the Elderly provides $10 monthly to a small group of elders ranging from 85 to 115 to help their families with their personal care. Contributions are also made to a scholarship program in the Gorongosa region of Mozambique and Clinique Monique, a child birthing clinic in Mali.

COMFORT OWUSU AND WOMENSTRUST. In 2006, Comfort Owusu approached WomensTrust for $55 to jumpstart her porridge business. Each morning, Comfort Owusu made four gallons of wheat porridge in a large pot, put it on her head and walked three miles from her home to the center of Pokuase and back, selling it as she went. A true entrepreneur, she noticed that there was no competition in her neighborhood for a prepared food business. So she started one of her own. Using several loans, she added a small eating establishment to her home with al fresco dining. In August 2007, Comfort Owusu opened the doors to her new restaurant, Fast Corner Chop Bar.

Never underestimate the power of women!

based life science companies. Prospective companies must demonstrate the concrete economic benefit to southwest Michigan that would result from any fund investment. In other words, companies accepting funding either have to be based in Kalamazoo, or relocate operating or headquarters units to the area. "The attorneys looked at us and said we were crazy," said Bill Johnston. "They didn't think you could force companies to come to a geographic area."

The fund set out to prove the doubters wrong. Southwest Michigan First was able to tap into public-minded investors, raising $50 million from limited partners – both individuals and institutions. As the *Financial Times* noted, the Southwest Michigan First Life Science Fund is "the largest sum of private capital ever to be raised and managed by an economic development organization."

The organizers believed the fund could succeed not simply by providing equity investment – after all, there are hundreds, if not thousands, of sources of capital – but because it could tap into Kalamazoo's existing commercial infrastructure. Positioned in Kalamazoo, the fund has access to a network of people and institutions able to provide crucial strategic advice to portfolio companies and a labor force of experienced scientists and life science executives. "To use a football analogy, we have the people who can carry the ball into the end zone," said Pat Morand, a former chief executive officer of three life science companies himself. "In southwest Michigan, we literally have everything you need to get from discovery to phase one trials to manufacturing to sales."

To ensure that the fund would invest in quality firms with solid prospects, Southwest Michigan First and Morand recruited a high-powered Scientific Advisory Board. "Our Scientific Advisory Board can be put up against any in the country," Pat Morand said proudly. Members include Göran Ando, M.D., a Specialist in General Medicine, the former head of research and development at Pharmacia and current Chairman of Novexel SA and Trigen Ltd.; Gregory Szpunar, Ph.D., Group Vice President of Global Project Management at Schering Plough and prior Chief Scientific Officer and Senior Vice President for research and development and manufacturing for Biovail Corporation; Gary Nabel, M.D., well known as a molecular virologist and immunologist for his work in the fields of HIV, cancer and Ebola virus research and the former head of the National Institutes of Health Vaccine Research Center; Doug Morton, Ph.D., formerly the Group Vice President of Technology Acquisitions & Operations for Discovery Research in Pharmacia; and James Richmond, a retired Senior Vice President for Global Marketing and Development for Stryker Corporation with a specialized background in finance, marketing and product engineering.

As it began to look for investments, the fund concentrated on its philosophy. Companies would need to have unique intellectual property, strong management, a marketable product and the possibility of an exit within three to five years. Initial investments would range from $500,000 to $3 million. A diversified portfolio of companies that could tap into the Kalamazoo region's human capital and physical infrastructure was desired in the areas of 1) agriculture, animal or human health and 2) diagnostic, device, therapeutic, service or medical manufacturing. "We're not going to populate our portfolio with one particular science, or one segment," said Pat Morand. "We're looking for science with commercial value."

In its first two years, the fund examined over 250 companies and made six investments. "We are not looking for volume, but quality," said Pat Morand. The portfolio companies operate in a range of life science-related industries and represent a mix of both homegrown firms and companies that have relocated to Kalamazoo to tap into the fund's capital and the region's human and physical resources.

The Southwest Michigan First Life Science Fund's first investment, in the summer of 2006, was a stake in NanoMed Pharmaceuticals. Founded in 2000 by faculty members of the University of Kentucky-College of Pharmacy, the company works on therapeutic and diagnostic products to treat or detect cancer and other serious diseases.

Its main development is a nanoparticle manufacturing technology used to formulate small molecules, peptides, proteins, plasmid DNA and diagnostic agents. When NanoMed closed its first round of funding, it announced it would relocate its corporate headquarters to the Michigan Technical Education Center, on the campus of Kalamazoo Valley Community College in the Groves Business Park. "Clearly, this is a very important milestone for NanoMed," said NanoMed Chief Executive Officer, Stephen Benoit, at the time. "We are honored to be the first company in the Southwest Michigan First Life Science Fund's portfolio."

The second investment was in EADevices. Founded in 2004, the company is developing the EANeedle, a device developed at Carnegie Mellon University that uses ultrasonic energy and thin, interchangeable needles to allow for less-invasive, early-stage biopsies. In December 2006, the company, which had won several business plan competitions, announced it had raised $1.3 million in seed funding, led by Southwest Michigan First and the Southwest Michigan First Life Science Fund, and would relocate to the Kalamazoo area.

InformMed, a device company founded in Peoria, Illinois, in 2001, became the fund's third portfolio company in April 2007. InformMed's flagship product is a hand-held pharmaceutical algorithm computerized calculator designed to prevent dosage errors in hospitals. The company closed a $2 million round of venture capital, led by the Southwest Michigan First Life Science Fund, and will use the funding to complete product development, continue its clinical study work and expand its executive management team. "Southwest Michigan First's life science expertise and extensive network of industry alliances are truly impressive, and we are fortunate to have them as our partner. The critical capital they bring, and the due diligence that preceded this financing round, validates the potential of our business model and solution in the health care industry," said Gary Conkright, Chief Executive Officer of InformMed. InformMed has since moved its Product Development and Operations Center to southwest Michigan.

In May 2007, Venomix, Inc., which is developing an insecticide based on spider venom, became the fund's fourth investment. The technology that Venomix is investigating was first developed at the University of Connecticut, but the company was created by a Michigan-based entrepreneur. "This is the second company I've started in Michigan. It's a great state for biotechnology start-ups and the people at the Southwest Michigan First Life Science Fund are extremely knowledgeable and helpful," said John McIntyre, the Chief Executive Officer of Venomix. As it sets up shop in the Southwest Michigan Innovation Center, the company is bringing two researchers from Calgary and Connecticut and plans to add technical staff. "The Southwest Michigan Innovation Center is the best organized and equipped incubation center that I have seen across the United States. Also, the quality of the other tenants was attractive," continued John McIntyre. "We look forward to developing many business relationships that will help us advance our technology rapidly."

> *All your dreams can come true if you have*
> *the courage to pursue them.*
>
> — WALT DISNEY

In January 2008, the Southwest Michigan First Life Science Fund announced its fifth and sixth investments. NephRx Corporation, already located in the Southwest Michigan Innovation Center, is developing two unique peptides, one for the treatment of acute renal failure and the second to treat diseases of the gastrointestinal tract. Metabolic Solutions Development Co. is formulating innovative therapeutics to treat diabetes and cardiovascular disease with novel treatments that will seek to free patients from adverse side effects and is partnering with Michigan-based scientific entrepreneurs in key business functions in their targeted discovery and development process. These latest investments show how two different companies with distinctive scientific

In the 1946 Frank Capra classic film, *It's a Wonderful Life*, Mr. Potter serves as the arch villain and antagonist of hero and resident "good guy" George Bailey. Mr. Potter is a heartless and greedy miser who makes George Bailey's life as penniless and miserable as possible. Mr. Potter's goal is to gain as much personal wealth as he can at everyone else's expense. In this film, Mr. Potter personifies yesterday's idea of big organizations – organizations seeking to make themselves profitable by "using" their employees and cheating their customers by offering the lowest quality products or services available. Today, there is a new vision of organizations and one that would make George Bailey proud.

MR. POTTER, THE "GEORGE BAILEYS" HAVE ARRIVED!

Traditionally, there have been three main sectors of organizations. The public sector focuses on government, the private on business and the social on non-profit or non-governmental issues. Over the past few decades, the lines separating these sectors have blurred and a fourth sector has emerged. This fourth sector is referred to as The Fourth Sector or the For-Benefit Sector. Organizations belonging to this fourth sector are oftentimes called For-Benefit Organizations.

For-Benefit Organizations are guided by a social purpose, are economically self-sufficient and endeavor to be socially, ethically and environmentally accountable. They embody the "best" characteristics of the other three sectors. Like the government sector, they look to be effective in solving public problems. Like the business sector, they can create jobs, economic stimulation and products and services for use by consumers. Like the social sector, they strive to address a wide range of societal issues.

For-Benefits endeavor to be democratic, inclusive, honest, responsible, transparent, collaborative, effective, ecologically aware and holistic. They seek to be the "ideal" organization. While looking to maximize the benefit to all stakeholders, they invest a majority of their economic profits to make the world a better place.

Altrushare Securities, based in Bridgeport, Connecticut, is an example of such an organization. At first glance, you see a typical Wall Street brokerage house, buying and selling stock, trading on the floor of the New York Stock Exchange. Upon closer inspection, you learn that two of its majority owners are charities, each with a one-third piece of the pie.

While traditional brokerage houses focus on corporate mergers, acquisitions, restructuring and underwriting, Altrushare focuses on community investment, or what they call Community Investment

Enterprise. Community Investment Enterprises are for-profit businesses created with the intent of improving the quality of life in low-income communities. For Altrushare Securities, the improvement comes in the fruition of youth, education and economic development programs within the undeserved communities themselves.

B Corporations are another type of Fourth Sector organization. B Corporations are corporations that meet or exceed comprehensive and transparent social and environmental performance standards, work to benefit stakeholders rather than shareholders and document this in their corporate governing documents and have a strong brand identity, one that exudes social awareness. An organization called B Lab has created "green," sustainable and socially accountable performance standards against which interested corporations are measured. Companies that "measure up" are then given another "brand" identity – the label of being a B Corporation – by the B Lab.

An example of a B Corporation is Give Something Back Business Products. This California-based office supplier donates half of its profits to community organizations chosen through an independent voting process of its customers and employees. Other B Corporation members include White Dog Café in Philadelphia, Pennsylvania, which offers menu items containing ingredients from local farms: Vermont-based Seventh Generation, which is the nation's leading distributer of non-toxic and environmentally safe household products; and UncommonGoods, an online and catalog retailer of uniquely crafted quality gifts.

Even conventional companies can make an impact in the Fourth Sector. In 2003, Goldman Sachs was commissioned by the United Nations to produce a report on its Environment Program Finance Initiative. The purpose of the report was to compare companies' financial performance in relation to such topics as energy emissions, health programs, safety practices and corporate governance. So popular was the report that Goldman Sachs now drafts comparable reports for the energy, food and beverage, media, mining and steel industries. Specifically for the energy industry, Goldman Sachs has created the Goldman Sachs Energy Environmental and Social Index, which ranks companies based upon environmental (i.e. climate change and pollution) and social (i.e. human rights, management diversity, future invest-ment, workforce, safety, transparency and vision) factors. Scoring well on these reports has become important to rated companies.

So who are the George Baileys leading these For-Benefit Organizations forward? It's the members of Generation Y (Gen Y). Let's consider those other generational terms and what they have come to signify first.

The Baby Boomers worked hard to achieve status, money and social grace. Generation X, considered by many to be overeducated under-achievers, worked to make the most money for doing as little possible. Now enter Gen Y.

Gen Y seeks not only compensation and traditional perks, but also a socially aware corporate culture and environment. Gen Y is concerned with the positive impact that they and the company that they chose to work for will make on society. More often than not, they select companies to work for that offer them the opportunity to contribute their professional and personal skills to charitable and volunteer organizations. Members of Gen Y feel personally responsible for society. And they expect the companies that they work for to help them do it.

The Fourth Sector and Gen Y are a match "made in heaven." George Bailey would have a field day!

property can qualify for investment from the fund: one is physically located in Kalamazoo presently; the other is committed to partnering with other Kalamazoo-based companies.

For the companies, money has only been part of the lure of the Southwest Michigan First Life Science Fund. As it invests, the fund takes board seats, typically two, on the company's board to provide advice and guidance. For example, Pat Morand now sits on the InformMed Board of Directors. Southwest Michigan First and the fund's Scientific Advisory Board help the portfolio companies recruit executives, professionals and outside board members and align them with local service providers as they grow and develop. In addition, the fund's uniquely positioned and committed network offers support services in the areas of industry expertise, regulatory strategy, reimbursement planning, exit strategies and early-stage business systems.

As previously discussed, venture capital, especially in its hot beds on the West Coast and in the Boston area, is a highly networked industry. Venture capital firms frequently work together with established groups of local investors and entrepreneurs to create a cluster, which in turn encourages spin-offs and more growth. In recent years, Kalamazoo has started to develop a similar network of venture capital investors centered on life science. Southwest Michigan First, the Kalamazoo Community Foundation and other local investors have helped form and invest in other venture capital funds that are either based in the area or have focused on it.

The Kalamazoo Community Foundation has become a committed investment player in business-related investments. In providing low-interest loans to several venture capital investment firms with the intention of boosting economic development in the greater Kalamazoo area, the foundation has been highly effective in making grants that have made a significant difference to recipient companies. One such recipient is NephRx, a biotechnology company dedicated to the discovery and development of therapeutic products for the treatment of kidney failure and disease. Founded in 2004, and based on technology from the University of Chicago, NephRx is now based in the Southwest Michigan Innovation Center and is committed to the community. More specifically, NephRx recruited its chief executive officer, treasurer and two main scientists from Kalamazoo.

The Southwest Michigan First Life Science Fund is 'the largest sum of private capital ever to be raised and managed by an economic development organization.'

- FINANCIAL TIMES

Teri Willey, Director of Cambridge Enterprise, the technology transfer group at Cambridge University, and an advisor to select technology and investment associations throughout the Midwest, gave high compliments to the Kalamazoo Community Foundation. "They didn't sit on their hands when everybody else was. NephRx needed to be in a community that understood product development," said Teri Willey. The company certainly got that in Kalamazoo.

The Kalamazoo Community Foundation's commitment to the community has not gone unnoticed. In October 2007, it was one of two community foundations named as a recipient of the Critical Impact Award from the Council on Foundations in Washington D.C. "In bestowing the 2007 Critical Impact Award on the Kalamazoo Community Foundation, we acknowledge its innovative leadership and bold vision in advancing the common good through effective grant making," stated Steve Gunderson, Chief Executive Officer of the Council on Foundations.

Another Kalamazoo capital venture was started in 2001 by Don Parfet, a member of the Upjohn family and a former senior executive at Pharmacia. He created the Apjohn Group, LLC, a health care business "accelerator" that helps launch companies. Don Parfet chose the name Apjohn as it is the Welsh spelling for Upjohn and to continue his family's commitment to the life science industry. Two years later, he helped put together the Kalamazoo-based $15 million Apjohn Ventures Fund, which invests in early-stage life science companies across the Midwest. The goal of the Apjohn Ventures Fund, simply said, is "to inspire life science entrepreneurs to build pharmaceutical successes much like Dr. William E. Upjohn did at the turn of the last century."

Although they are two separate entities, the Apjohn Group and Apjohn Ventures Fund work together. The Apjohn Group is an accomplished team of experienced business and pharmaceutical profes-sionals skilled in launching life science companies. Its focus is on early-stage life science opportunities, with a primary concentration on biopharmaceuticals, which hold the promise of new medical treatment or diagnostic breakthroughs. The partners comprising the Apjohn Group have extensive knowledge and networks in all phases of the drug development process, from discovery to commercialization to operational leadership. Their objective is to accelerate and enhance value for their portfolio companies by bridging the management and financial gap between innovators and the marketplace, as well as to achieve key early-stage milestones in the product development process.

The preferred business arrangement for Apjohn Group is to take on substantial upfront risk by assuming an equity position in a newly formed company in exchange for management leadership and services. Opportunities are often obtained by referrals or through interactions with university technology officers and academic scientists. The Apjohn Group is connected with local and national angel investors, venture capital firms interested specifically in life science and the Apjohn Ventures Fund.

The Apjohn Ventures Fund is a venture capital fund established to invest primarily in early-stage life science companies across the Midwest. The goal of the fund is to provide investors with superior financial returns by making equity investments in innovative life science companies with sustainable and outstanding growth potential. It is one of the few venture firms in Michigan and in the Midwest with experience and focus in biotech investing within the life science sector. The attractions of the fund to potential companies and investors alike include the fund's depth of pharmaceutical and biotech industry expertise and networks, strategic business perspective, operational and financial expertise, syndication deal experience with angels and regional and national venture capital funds, mergers and acquisitions and initial public offering background and its relationship with the Apjohn Group.

One of the Apjohn Group's success stories is Afmedica, a privately held, drug-coated device company formed in Kalamazoo in 2002. The success of Afmedica goes to show how intertwined a life science community can be. In 2002, the Apjohn Group provided Afmedica with business and scientific talent during the company's first 18 months. This led to a successful launch and raising of the first rounds of capital. Afmedica was also backed by TGap Ventures, a Kalamazoo-based venture capital fund that makes initial investments between $250,000 and $1 million and typically co-invests with several other venture capitalists. TGap Ventures focuses primarily on early-stage investments throughout the Midwest, concentrating on medical devices,

Imagine being in your 80s and still gainfully employed. Imagine being in your 80s and riding your bike to work every day. Imagine being in your 80s, being a millionaire and living off of Social Security and your wife's modest pension. Imagine being in your 80s and giving away all the profits made from the company that you have founded to a charitable organization each year. Imagine being Hal Taussig...

A "HAND UP, NOT A HAND OUT"

At age 33, Hal Taussig found himself broke. He had just lost everything he had in the family cattle-ranching business. To support his family, Hal Taussig immediately shifted into the education field. While earning a Ph.D. in American Civilization at the University of Pennsylvania in 1965, Hal Taussig taught classes at the middle and high schools levels. Upon graduation, he landed a tenure-track position at Spalding College (now Spalding University) in Kentucky. Hal Taussig's do-gooder nature took charge. After supporting a liberalized curriculum over the objections of the institution's president and deans, he found himself unemployed again at the age of 45.

Hal Taussig had decided to take a family sabbatical tour of Europe before his dismissal. While overseas, Hal learned that tradition provided the Europeans with a stronger sense of community. This realization would soon come to personify his life.

Upon arriving back home, Hal Taussig wrote *The Shoestring Sabbatical*, a guide to getting teachers around Europe cheap. Although geared toward teachers, travelers of all professions started calling him for information. Hal Taussig had an idea. Borrowing $5,000 from a friend in 1975, he started Untours – a travel agency for the un-vacation. The premise was simple. Untours would set up a traveler for two weeks or more in an apartment in a local European community. The traveler would then live locally and – maybe even work – as a local European resident. Breakfast at a neighborhood *boulangerie* rather than at the Ritz would be the norm.

With destinations in more than 20 countries around the globe, Untours generates annual sales of more than $8 million even though it does no advertising. More than 40 percent of customers are repeat clients and the rest come via word of mouth.

More impressive than the growth is what Untours does with its profits. For the first decade, Hal Taussig paid all employees, including himself, the same wage. This policy was based upon Hal Taussig's strong beliefs in equality and justice. Today, Untours' employees make about 20 percent above the industry average and its company policy is that the highest-paid employee can earn no more than four times the salary of the lowest-paid.

In 1992, after years of supporting good causes out of his own pocketbook, Hal Taussig founded the Untours Foundation. All after-tax profits from Untours go into the foundation. Inspired by the Grameen Bank in Bangladesh, which makes microloans to local women who plan to start business ventures in order to support themselves, the Untours Foundation offers loans at 2 percent interest as a "hand up, not a hand out." Most projects originate in the progressive business circles in which Hal Taussig travels or from entrepreneurs who approach him directly. Donated funds must be used to create jobs, build low-income housing or support fair trade products – products where the providers and workers earn a fair price and wage, consumers receive superior goods and land is farmed in a sustainable way.

Recipients include the Home Care Associates of Philadelphia, a worker-owned cooperative of former welfare recipients, which offers quality home health care; the Landless Workers Movement of Brazil, which has aided over a million Brazilian farmers in creating a self-sufficient farming lifestyle; Belu Spring Water of London, England, which boasts a corn-based biodegradable bottle; and ShoreBank, Rehab CDs, a full-scale bank committed to investing in low-income areas of Chicago.

So positive is the organization that failures are even looked at in a constructive manner. Hal Taussig once lost the $400,000 that he had invested in a Philadelphia-based used-clothing recycler called New Threads due to a crash in the used-clothing market and management issues. He considers as successes the fact that the company employed over 70 people in its four-year stint, many of them homeless, and that they all found jobs elsewhere afterwards based on their skills learned on-the-job.

Ever a fair employer, Hal Taussig still struggles with being generous to his staff and his mission to help the poor. "The higher the salaries we pay, the less money we have to give away..."

Imagine being in your 80s and being that generous.

software, specialty manufacturing, Internet, telecommunications, health care and other high-growth companies. The Kalamazoo Community Foundation is also an investor in TGap.

The Afmedica investment was successfully exited in October 2005 when it was acquired by Angiotech Pharmaceuticals, Inc., a publicly traded company in Vancouver, British Columbia. But the Afmedica story doesn't stop there. In 2005, Afmedica spun out another company, MedElute, Inc. MedElute is a preclinical-stage, drug-eluting materials company focused on treating post-surgical adhesions using a highly novel anti-platelet approach. MedElute, now based in Kalamazoo, is backed by the Apjohn Group, Apjohn Ventures, TGap Partners and several other co-investors. The growth and investment cycle has begun again.

These funds, along with many of their investors, seek a dual bottom line. They want to gain a return on capital invested while encouraging local economic growth. "We're limited partners in all four of the local venture capital funds, with the hope that over time they will cause this region to become a hotbed of entrepreneurship, and a place for companies to land with financial support to help them move from the early stages through development," said Jack Hopkins. But Kalamazoo is also careful in its investments, continually seeking quality over quantity.

Venture capital funds tap into a vital but limited pool of high net worth investors. And they generally have a higher threshold for investment, seeking to make minimum investments of $1 million to $1.5 million. But many companies need smaller amounts to get started, anywhere from $200,000 to $500,000. And in a community like Kalamazoo, there are multiple sources of wealth, and hence a potentially broader base of investors interested in and willing to back start-up companies seeking smaller amounts of funds. "If we can get an experienced angel investor group of 40 to 50 people, we'll be in a good situation," said Paul Neeb, Vice President at Southwest Michigan First, who spends most of his time looking at life science opportunities. "And this would be something that complements the Southwest Michigan First Life Science Fund."

If the majority of people were right, the majority of people would be rich.

- RON ELENBAAS

To tap into this potential, Southwest Michigan First in October 2006 launched First Angels, an angel investor network geared toward making financial and intellectual capital available to growing companies in the Kalamazoo area in a range of industries. As is the case with the Southwest Michigan First Life Science Fund, First Angels has a dual bottom line, seeking returns *and* economic development. Just as the Southwest Michigan First Life Science Fund provides synergies with the community, the First Angels network seeks to tap into the region's growing start-up culture. Ideas for investments are generated by referrals from Southwest Michigan First, the Southwest Michigan First Life Science Fund, Western Michigan University's Biosciences Research and Commercialization Center at Western Michigan University and other local investment groups.

A not-for-profit organization, First Angels is led by its members who evaluate prospective companies to determine if they're ready for funding. Companies that pass the screening are invited to make a 30-minute presentation to members of the First Angels' group at one of its monthly meetings. If investors are interested, they form a team to conduct due diligence and make an investment recommendation to the group. Each individual member can then decide whether or not to participate.

Set against the losses the community has endured in recent years – the reduction of the paper mills, the closure of the General Motors' plant and the rounds of cutbacks at Pfizer – these efforts, a $1 million investment here, the creation of four new jobs there, even if they are high-paying jobs, may seem like drops in the bucket. But they are not. They are creating the future. To date, 26 companies and more than 2,000 jobs have been created in Kalamazoo as a result of these efforts. And Kalamazoo is confident that more are to come.

The idea is to build a culture of investing, a culture of growth, a culture of wealth creation.

– PAT MORAND

More importantly, the capital now available in Kalamazoo has created an infrastructure for entrepreneurship, which is a key ingredient for long-term growth. Some of the companies backed by the funds and some of the start-ups in the incubator may fail. Others might be sold to out-of-town companies as they evolve and succeed. Either way, however, the development is seen as a win for the community. "If we do things correctly, we'll keep new companies pushing to that stage where they can be acquired," said Pat Morand. "The idea is to build a culture of investing, a culture of growth, a culture of wealth creation."

Venture capital funds deploy the cash raised from successful exits into new ventures. So do the entrepreneurs who do so. Over a 10-year period, it's not hard to imagine that one of the start-ups seeking a small investment from the Southwest Michigan First Life Science Fund, or one of the entrepreneurs making a pitch at next month's First Angels meeting, could develop into a major employer and a contributing corporate citizen. More significantly, when a community expresses a willingness to invest funds in its own future, positive results always follow.

CHAPTER 3

INFRASTRUCTURE: BRICKS AND MORTAR

Believe it can be done.
When you believe something can be done,
really believe, your mind will find the ways to do it.
Believing a solution paves the way to solution.

— DAVID SCHWARTZ

While the 21st century economy is characterized by high-speed information, creative thought processes and competitive research and development, bricks and mortar still matter a great deal.

All companies need physical space in which to operate. And that space must epitomize a company's mission, strategy and self-identity. The businesses that made Kalamazoo may have started in garages or home workshops. But for contemporary entrepreneurs in life science, technology and manufacturing, a state-of-the-art space in which to work is crucial for early development. In addition, having spaces in which groups of like-minded people can meet and exchange ideas is vital.

In the 21st century economy, industry sectors also tend to develop in clusters. Successful industries cannot grow independently of their suppliers, their talent pools or even their competitors. Strength clearly lies in numbers. And so a community that wishes to build a globally relevant industry sector must create an atmosphere in which one company that has encountered an issue can share information with another company encountering a similar issue.

But when the Kalamazoo area began to encounter challenges in the late 1990s, the region lacked such space. Most of the innovation and research to date had taken place in Upjohn's expensive, state-of-the-art laboratories. Then, after Pharmacia merged with Upjohn, the company began to scale back its research and development presence in downtown Kalamazoo. It was evident that the region lacked a start-up culture. And it was becoming increasingly evident that the community lacked places where start-ups – especially those in life science – could congregate.

Fortunately for Kalamazoo, a set of circumstances and fortuitous and forward thinking led to the creation of an important new piece of business infrastructure.

In the late 1990s, as Kalamazoo's economy was taking a downturn, Western Michigan University's rapidly growing College of Engineering and Applied Sciences, which had outgrown its campus, was a bright spot. "Our college of engineering was one of the fastest growing over the last 20 years," said Bob Miller, Western Michigan University Associate Vice President of Community Outreach. "The need was really there for a facility of its own."

One natural area to expand was the former Lee Baker Farm, southwest of downtown. Residents of the nearby Parkview Hills neighborhood earlier in the decade had rejected a development plan for the area due to concerns about traffic congestion and the loss of green space. But now, other area communities were offering to help Western Michigan University build its engineering campus if it would relocate. The struggle over the college's future – and the desire to raise funds to help Western Michigan University keep its engineering college in Kalamazoo – spurred action.

At the time, recalled Bob Brown, President of Arcadia Capital Corporation, President of the Monroe-Brown Foundation and a founder of Southwest Michigan First, the community had committed funds for a Michigan Technical Education Center, one in a group of buildings located throughout Michigan that provides incubator spaces for high-growth companies and workforce training. Land near I-94 was acquired and the technical training facility was planned on the campus of Kalamazoo Valley Community College.

In order to handle both the Michigan Technical Education Center initiative and address the need to keep Western Michigan University's College of Engineering and Applied Sciences in Kalamazoo, a group of area business leaders led by Bob Brown; Craig DeNooyer, President of Treystar Holdings; and Marilyn Schlack, President of Kalamazoo Valley Community College, formed Southwest Michigan First in 1999. Southwest Michigan First would be a privately funded not-for-profit economic development organization designed to stimulate economic growth across the Kalamazoo region. Southwest Michigan First would be responsible for attracting new business to the area, helping existing area businesses to expand, addressing issues pertaining to the retention of these businesses and creating job growth.

The newly formed body was committed to raising funds for these projects, including $15 million for the engineering school. Through extensive efforts, which included as Bob Brown put it, "screaming and banging on desks," the funds were raised and Western Michigan University's College of Engineering and Applied Sciences decided to stay in Kalamazoo.

The plans were expanded and the engineering school was to be surrounded by an entire technology and research park. "The idea was to build a business technology park as part of this expansion to enable companies and the college to collaborate more closely," said Bob Miller. The entire venture was now to be called the Western Michigan University Business Technology and Research Park.

In the fall of 1999, ground was broken on the Business Technology and Research Park. The office park was intended to bring a range of benefits to the community. Built in an environmentally sensitive manner, it contained 70 acres of passive and recreational landscape.

For centuries, flour mills were usually water-powered, although some used wind or livestock to turn wheels in tandem to move grain where it needed to go. A wooden drum mechanism wound by a chain hoisted sacks of grain to the top of the mill house to be emptied into bins. Next, the grain was poured down a hopper to be stoned into flour on the meal floor below. Sloping grooves in the floor boards helped pass the flour down a chute to be collected again in sacks now ready for shipment.

FROM SEEDS TO SCIENCE

From 1920 to 2000, such a flour mill was located at 524 North Boonville Avenue, Springfield, Missouri and was responsible for feeding much of the rural Midwest. But since May 30, 2007, a much different facility is located on that spot and providing a much different "fodder."

Today, the wheels that turn on the site are no longer made of wood. They are the wheels of clever minds working to feed the world as a result of applied research in the areas of nanotechnology, bio-materials, advanced technologies, genomics/proteomics, bio-systems software engineering and biomedical instrument development.

When Missouri State University decided to create both a research hub where it could team with corporate partners on applied research projects and hands-on interactive classrooms in 2005, the university chose not to look to outlying suburban areas. Instead it focused on downtown Springfield's historic industrial area, previously occupied by the Missouri Farmers Association feed mill. This brownfield site was rid of PCB-containing transformers, grain fumigants used in conjunction with the flour mill's operation and groundwater contamination. In its place, a gleaming brick and glass seven-story edifice was erected. Heralded as one of the most significant redevelopment projects in Springfield's history, the resulting Roy Blunt Jordan Valley Innovation Center is intended to provide revitalization to the downtown area and bring coveted higher-paying jobs as well as new residents to the downtown area.

The building was christened the Roy Blunt Jordan Valley Innovation Center in honor of U.S. Congressman Roy Blunt's persistent efforts to secure federal funds to assist in the facility's renovation. The U.S. Department of Defense contributed $12 million to Phase I of the project, which established the building with its advanced research and development laboratories. It contributed an additional $2.6 million towards Phase II for an advanced manufacturing and rapid prototyping facility.

The site boasts three departments, each with its own mission for promoting Missouri-based businesses. The Center for Applied Science and Engineering is committed to the development and support of advanced materials research industries with a focus on carbon-based electronics and devices, materials research and characterization and various micro electro-mechanical sensors and systems fabrication. The Center for BioMedical and Life Sciences is focused on the development and support of advanced biotechnology industries targeting medical instruments and materials, bio-processing techniques and equipment, agribusiness research and development and chem/bio sensors and systems. Lastly, Springfield Innovation Inc. supports advanced product development and technology-based entrepreneurs in order to make Missouri-based industries more competitive while providing interdisciplinary work experiences for Missouri State University students. In addition, senior corporate affiliates occupy offices and lab space on four floors of the building.

What the Roy Blunt Jordan Valley Innovation Center itself has done is remarkable – not only creating a haven for research and jobs but also helping to redefine a city. But it doesn't stop there. The facility is achieving secondary goals too. Other companies have relocated to the area to be close to what is going on there. Among them, U.S. Photonics, which specializes in micro- and nano-machining, is moving across the street. Also, students and faculty members from Missouri State University are sticking around. Now, they don't have to go off to other markets in search of high-paying jobs. Approximately 95 percent of the research staff in the facility is composed of the university's students or previous students. About 50 percent of the hundreds of jobs posted on the university's Career Center database are related to work being done at the Roy Blunt Jordan Valley Innovation Center.

Unlike the simple wheel, water and chain methods of years gone by, the site now houses a multi-million dollar robotics line amongst other things. Mechanical parts forming a kinematic chain comprised of links, actuators and joints automate the process of coating canopies for U.S. Navy jet cockpits in order to increase their longevity. The interactions between nerve and glial cells are being monitored to determine what signals the brain to sense pain brought on by temporomandibular joint disorders. Scientists are investigating whether hydrogen peroxide is biologically useful in an anti-terrorism project.

So, from seeds to science. From grain to brownfield revitalization. From flour sacks to technology. From silos to jobs. One Springfield, Missouri site has changed to keep up with the times. That's some food for thought.

In 2003, the Business Technology and Research Park welcomed its first corporate tenant, Richard-Allan Scientific (now Thermo Fisher Scientific), a company that makes instruments and supplies for anatomical pathology. While establishing the Business Technology and Research Park as an outlet for growth was important, the community clearly needed a place where the next Richard-Allan Scientifics (and the next Upjohns and Strykers) could find space and support. The changes afoot in the pharmaceutical industry – the mergers, the downsizing of corporate research and the growing reliance of Big Pharma on small entrepreneurial companies for discovery research – were a cause of concern in Kalamazoo. As Bill Johnston put it, "We had a 100-year legacy of commercializing pharmaceutical compounds, and we were within one working generation of losing that skill set."

We had a 100-year legacy of commercializing pharmaceutical compounds, and we were within one working generation of losing that skill set.

– BILL JOHNSTON

The region clearly had the "software" – the scientists – especially as Pfizer began to diversify its research operations away from Kalamazoo. But it needed the "hardware" – office space and, especially, wet lab facilities that life science companies required. As if they had a crystal ball, Southwest Michigan First saw the need before it was actually there. "Big pharmaceutical companies, like Pfizer (and Upjohn and Pharmacia before them), which were cutting out research and engineering expertise, would have to outsource," said Barry Broome, the first Chief Executive Officer of Southwest Michigan First. If Kalamazoo could build a place where small local start-ups could set up shop, they could begin to provide services to Pfizer, and ultimately, to other companies – and create a new life science cluster.

The notion of building a life science incubator quickly found widespread support. After all, Dr. Homer Stryker had started his research in a workshop in Borgess Hospital's basement, and look what he achieved. Imagine if a group of bright minds had state-of-the-art facilities available to them.

Western Michigan University agreed to donate 15 acres of land in the Business Technology and Research Park. Southwest Michigan First appealed to Chuck Perricone, the Speaker of the Michigan House of Representatives, who was from Kalamazoo. Through Speaker Chuck Perricone's effort, the state of Michigan agreed to contribute $5 million. And the Kalamazoo Community Foundation extended a $2 million low-interest loan. Southwest Michigan First through its partnership with the city of Kalamazoo, Kalamazoo County and other local philanthropists, including the Gilmore Foundation, raised funds for construction of the 58,000-square-foot, $13 million incubator/accelerator. "We built it thinking it would be a Noah's Ark for talent, thinking smart people would come here if we showed the courage to go as far as we could," said Barry Broome.

The Southwest Michigan Innovation Center opened in April 2003. And the timing was propitious. In July 2002, Pfizer had announced a deal to merge with Pharmacia, which at the time employed 6,300 people in the Kalamazoo area and another 1,000 contract workers in Kalamazoo County. In April 2003, Pfizer decided to transfer research and development operations from Kalamazoo, moving jobs to Connecticut and California. The job loss for Kalamazoo: 1,200.

The announcements were a huge shock and represented a major loss. But there was now infrastructure in place to help recover. The natural concern was that the community would lose its human capital – that all the scientists rendered jobless would leave. Southwest Michigan First launched a public relations campaign – dubbed the Stick Around Campaign – to encourage former Pfizer employees to start their own businesses. Pfizer agreed to keep some research and

What do you say when a wealthy philanthropist offers your emerging university of roughly 9,000 students $25 million? "It is not enough!"

MAKING THE WORLD A BETTER PLACE - NOT BY LAND, BUT BY SEA!

That may seem unbelievable, but that is exactly what Dr. Robert R. Furgason, President of Texas A&M-Corpus Christi, told retired publisher Ed Harte. He must have said it nicely though, because Ed Harte reconsidered and responded with $46 million for the establishment of the Harte Research Institute for Gulf of Mexico Studies.

Ed Harte's gift was noteworthy not only because of its size, but also because he created the best-funded marine science center in the nation with one stroke of the pen.

What would inspire a lifelong newspaper man to fund a marine science institute whose mandate is "Make a Difference?" Actually, "who" is the question not "what". *The New York Times* refers to her as "Her Deepness" and the Library of Congress calls her a "Living Legend." She is the first recipient of the Hero of the Planet Award and she is America's oceanographer – she is Sylvia Earle.

It was the good fortune of Texas A&M-Corpus Christi, and indeed all who love the Gulf of Mexico, that Harte, read *Sea Change: A Message of the Oceans*, Sylvia Earle's 1995 tome on our planet's oceans. Ed Harte became convinced that there was much to be learned by studying one of the last great unexplored regions on the planet – the Gulf of Mexico. The Harte Research Institute was born.

Along with Ed Harte's endowment, the state of Texas funded an $18 million research center overlooking Corpus Christi Bay. Completed in 2005, the building has 10 wet and dry labs, a teaching laboratory, a dive locker, conference center and offices to house the institute's six endowed chairs, their staffs, students and visiting researchers from Mexico and Cuba, nations that also have a lot at stake in ensuring the sustainability of the Gulf of Mexico and immediately addressing the issues of overfishing, pollution and coastal habitat loss.

The institute's endowed chairs read like a "who's who" in marine policy and science and they oversee areas of specialty as broad as marine policy and law to biodiversity and conservation. All programs are focused on the Gulf of Mexico. In addition, the institute is moving forward with plans to do what has never been done before: inventorying every species in the Gulf of Mexico and documenting its habitat and status.

As the nation's top marine science center, the Harte Research Institute will chart the course of the future of the Gulf of Mexico. Its researchers will undoubtedly discover new species, craft new environmental policies and bridge both scientific and political chasms that exist between the United States, Mexico and Cuba. The delicate balance of nature and its contribution to continental economies and ecosystems will hopefully be protected - thus making the world a better place.

All because one man who created wealth and then decided to give it away read a book written by a lady who discovered a passion for the sea as a child and then talked to a college president who challenged him to do more.

development in the area, as well as animal health, manufacturing and an applied chemical testing facility downtown. Also, Pfizer pledged to donate millions of dollars worth of equipment. The state of Michigan loaned $2 million to help former employees become entrepreneurs.

*Vision is the painting of a picture
that brings passion in people.*

— BILL HYBELS

In addition, the state of Michigan helped with $10 million to develop Western Michigan University's Bioscience Research and Commercialization Center within the Southwest Michigan Innovation Center. The Bioscience Research and Commercialization Center is a commercially focused and science-driven translational research center dedicated to using its pharmaceutical expertise and resources to the commercialization of promising life science discoveries and the growth of Michigan's life science business sector.

The Southwest Michigan Innovation Center became a natural place for the process of regeneration to begin. It would now be a haven for scientists who had spent their careers at Upjohn, and later Pharmacia and Pfizer, to continue their legacy of innovation close to home. Dr. Doug Morton, a 30-year Upjohn/ Pharmacia veteran, returned to Kalamazoo in November 2003 to serve as Chief Executive Officer. Empty when it opened, the Southwest Michigan Innovation Center began to fill up with one- and two-person operations, many of them started by former Upjohn/Pharmacia/Pfizer employees. Most of the companies that launched in 2003 were service-based companies, like Kalexsyn, Inc., a medicinal chemistry contract research firm, and PharmOptima, which provides consulting and laboratory services in the area of drug discovery for cardiovascular, central nervous system, cancer, dermatology and infectious diseases.

There were good financial reasons for start-ups to locate in the incubator. Since the Business Technology and Research Park was a Michigan Smart Zone, tenants would receive breaks on taxes. Rent in the incubator was subsidized, although it was set to rise over a three-year period. And in some instances, Southwest Michigan First provided forgivable loans to help companies finish lab space.

But more important than the money was the space, services and interaction that could take place there. Common lunch and meeting rooms provided networking opportunities. Most of those setting up shop in the incubator were career scientists who decided later in life to become entrepreneurs. Many of those scientists were reluctant entrepreneurs who wanted to stay in the area. They wanted to build something, yet they didn't know how they were going to raise money. Access to the state-of-the-art wet labs was vital. "But we wanted to layer that with training and mentoring them as time went on so that they became more and more knowledgeable about business," said Dr. Doug Morton. "They're all very smart and capable people from a scientific point of view. But they didn't have the business experience."

Just as constructing the Southwest Michigan Innovation Center was a joint venture between government, corporations and the community, so was the effort to construct a latticework of support. Southwest Michigan First assembled a preferred supplier database of accountants and lawyers for the start-ups, and brought in consultants to help them write business plans.

Since 2003, many of the companies have grown from ideas into thriving small companies. CeeTox, which does in vitro toxicity screening of potential drug candidates and chemicals, started in July 2003. The eight-person firm has analyzed more than 4,000 new chemical entities. ADMETRx, another of those companies, seeks to improve decision-making in drug discovery by providing high-quality ADME (absorption, distribution, metabolism and excretion) profiling to guide in the selection of developable drug candidates.

No power of government is as formidable a force for the good as the creativity and entrepreneurial drive of the American people.

— RONALD REAGAN

Four of the original tenants have graduated. AureoGen Biosciences, in October 2006, relocated to a 4,000-square-foot space about five miles away. PharmOptima, a pre-clinical research and discovery company founded in 2003, having seen its workforce grow from 10 to potentially 35 by the end of 2007, announced plans in February 2007 to move to its own 10,000-square-foot facility in nearby Portage Commerce Park. The following month, Kalexsyn broke ground on a new 20,000-square-foot building in the Business Technology and Research Park, which would allow it to boost its staff from 23 to 32.

In the spring of 2007, the incubator was fully occupied by 14 companies, most of which were founded by former Pfizer scientists, employing more than 200 people. And the organic process of incubation, growth, graduation and renewal continues. In June 2007, Venomix, a start-up that makes insecticide products based on spider-venom peptides, became the newest tenant. Emiliem, an oncology drug development company, soon thereafter announced that it would relocate its research and development center from Emeryville, California to the Southwest Michigan Innovation Center.

The double helix shape has come to be associated strongly with deoxyribonucleic acid (DNA) in modern popular culture. The image is basically two congruent helices that are joined along an axis to form a chain. The "double" image allows one to picture the reproduction capability of DNA, considered to be the foundation of life, and its strength due to the fact that the two intertwining helices cannot be pulled apart.

CAN A BUILDING BECOME THE DNA OF A LOCAL ECONOMY?

The study of DNA has led to a multitude of advancements in science that have resulted in the betterment of health and the human condition. DNA studies are performed at institutions around the globe. The Scripps Research Institute, one of the United States' largest, private, non-profit research organizations, is not only one of those institutions, but is also one that unequivocally stands out in the area of biomedical science.

Founded as Scripps Metabolic Clinic in 1924, in La Jolla, California, a suburb of San Diego, the Scripps Research Institute and its scientists are actively investigating the biological and chemical aspects of more than 40 diseases, including AIDS, Alzheimer's, cancer, multiple sclerosis, Sjogren's syndrome and sleep disorders. Funded by the National Institutes of Health and other federal agencies, the institute employs the finest minds in the biosciences field and provides them with cutting-edge laboratories and equipment. The resulting scientific research crosses disease lines and considers the structure and function of proteins; biocatalysis and protein design; the causes and regulation of inflammation; and the structure and function of plant and animal cells.

Since its foundation, the Scripps Research Institute is credited with intertwining itself into the San Diego region and transforming it from a tourist and military town to a world center for biotechnology. Following Scripps, Jonas Salk, discoverer of the polio vaccine, founded his Salk Institute there. Additionally, the Burnham Institute, specializing in cancer research, followed suit. Along with the University of California at San Diego, those three institutes have spawned nearly 500 biotech companies that have grown around what is considered to be the nation's third-rated biotech center.

In 2003, the Scripps Research Institute began considering an expansion that would focus on biomedical research, technology development and drug design. At the same time, Florida Governor Jeb Bush began to develop a new vision for the state of Florida. Governor Jeb Bush desired to diversify the economy of his state and give it a stronger foundation for the future. He wanted something defining that would create a clustering effect around a forward-thinking industry and both draw companies and create high-paying jobs.

Considering that Florida is the fourth largest populated state and ranks third in the consumption of medical and health care products, Governor Jeb Bush focused his attention on biotechnology and, more specifically, the new location of the Scripps Research Institute. Using a variety of incentives, a $310 million package crafted by the Florida legislature for equipment and staffing and an additional $200 million from Palm Beach County for land and buildings, Governor Jeb Bush lured the Scripps Research Institute and got it to commit to a site in Palm Beach, Florida.

The Jupiter campus of Florida Atlantic University was selected and construction was immediately undertaken. Scheduled for completion in early 2009, three buildings totaling 350,000 square feet will house state-of-the-art laboratories, world-renowned biomedical researchers and administrative offices. Amongst the technological advancements located there will be a robot that has the capability to screen 250,000 to 1,000,000 chemical compounds in a day at the cost of a dime per compound, one of only five in the country.

The state of Florida hopes to achieve its own "helix" effect and have an intertwining community impact like the one achieved in San Diego. Within 15 years, it is predicted that the site will generate 6,500 direct jobs, an additional 40,000 from biotech spinoffs and company relocations and $3.2 billion toward the state's gross domestic product. To that end, the German research giant, the Max Planck Society, has already committed a bio-imaging center. Also, IBM has partnered with Scripps Florida on "Project Check-mate," an advanced research project on pandemic viruses. Governor Jeb Bush has likened the potential influx of intellectual energy from Scripps Florida on the Florida economy to what Henry Flagler's railroad, air conditioning, the Kennedy Space Center and Walt Disney World have done for it.

As a testament to Florida's hope and financial commitment, a lattice-shaped spire constructed of steel tubes and capable of withstanding wind gusts of over 140 miles per hour sits atop the central building at the site and the headquarters of Scripps Florida. The design of the spire is meant to evoke an image of the upward-swirling double helix of DNA. And, it is a harbinger of the promise of good things to come for Scripps Florida and the state's future economy.

More broadly, the Business Technology and Research Park has emerged as an important new business center, with a total of 30 companies employing about 600 people. The public investments that started as a $37 million effort to create a new engineering college have been leveraged into a continuing project that represents more than $160 million in investment. In addition to attracting life science companies, the Business Technology and Research Park has created concentrations in other industries, which in turn, help attract other businesses. There are 11 advanced engineering firms in the Business Technology and Research Park, for example. So when Soil & Material Engineers, Inc., a civil engineering firm, wanted to open an office in West Michigan, it made sense for it to choose the Business Technology and Research Park.

The Business Technology and Research Park also functions as a magnet for local companies. TEKNA Solutions, an industrial design firm that specializes in medical devices and was founded by the Western Michigan University alumni husband-and-wife team of Kris and Claire Eager, has built a 24,000-square-foot building at the park. Blue Granite, an information technology company founded by young Western Michigan University graduates, arrived in 2004.

The buildings in the Business Technology and Research Park and the Southwest Michigan Innovation Center, and the companies that operate in them, may seem futuristic and relentlessly forward-looking. But the ethos and the idea behind creating these incubators of new business in Kalamazoo is more a matter of going back to the future. "Dr. William E. Upjohn and Dr. Homer Stryker needed lab space," said Jack Hopkins. "If we can help encourage entrepreneurialism, company and job creation and good sustainable jobs, growing companies will lead to wealth creation and that leads to philanthropy. The cycle that Upjohn and Stryker created will go on and on."

The Business Technology and Research Park and the Southwest Michigan Innovation Center represented the creation of vital new business infrastructure from scratch in order to make the best possible use of an existing resource – the community's scientists and life science professionals. Eleven miles away, entrepreneurs transformed the region's largest single piece of existing physical business infrastructure into a building that can also house growing businesses.

In 1992, General Motors announced that it planned to close its massive, 2.2-million-square-foot stamping plant on the outskirts of Kalamazoo. At its peak, the plant, which sits on 340 acres heading south from downtown, employed 4,500 people. But as General Motors retrenched and diversified, the plant joined the growing list of operations to be decommissioned. When the lights went out on June 30, 1999, David Smith and his colleagues at Hackman Capital, a Los Angeles-based design and real estate firm, found themselves the new owners of 165 stamping presses and "35 years of accumulation of everything from file cabinets to coffee pots."

If we can help encourage entrepreneurialism, company and job creation and good sustainable jobs, growing companies will lead to wealth creation and that leads to philanthropy. The cycle that Upjohn and Stryker created will go on and on.

– JACK HOPKINS

The plant, like many others abandoned by auto makers throughout the Midwest, could have simply been shuttered, or demolished. But Smith and his colleagues saw potential. Their initial plan was to find a tenant in the automotive industry that could use the equipment in place. When that didn't pan out, they sold the equipment, secured long-term financing and began to re-imagine the project as a distribution and logistics center that would anchor a larger mixed-use development; Midlink Business Park was born. "We didn't want it to be the old General Motors building," said David Smith. It definitely no longer is.

Located on I-94, about midway between Chicago and Detroit, with convenient and excellent highway access to cities throughout the Midwest, the site made perfect sense for a distribution center. Other companies had recognized the advantages of locating such operations in the area, including the Target and Wal-Mart distribution centers, so the potential was there. The new owners invested about $30 million to revamp the building, splitting it into two institutional-quality buildings, removing 700 tons of scrap steel and 300,000 square feet of space and creating a truck plaza in between Midlink East and Midlink West.

Southwest Michigan First and the Michigan Economic Development Corporation helped Midlink secure a Renaissance Zone as of January 1, 2000 for part of the 340-acre site, which would free a majority of the tenants of most local and state taxes until 2017. For tenants using the space as a warehouse, the savings can amount to 75 cents to $1 per square foot per year on building rates that range from $3 to $4 per square foot. Midlink also received assistance from the community – the Charter Township of Comstock invested all tax revenues through 2017 through the Renaissance Zone program and the Michigan Economic Development Corporation assisted with a $3 million public infrastructure grant which was used to build two miles of public roads and utilities.

In February 2005, Midlink, reborn as a 1.9-million-square-foot facility divisible to 25,000 square feet, signed its first tenant – International Component Strategies, a reseller of auto parts that was founded by Joe Cortes, the son of a former controller at Upjohn. Since January 1, 2005, Midlink has leased more than 1.5 million square feet of space to a wide range of tenants. Erickson's Flooring & Supply Company has taken space for distribution. Electrolux, which makes refrigerators, leased 700,000 square feet to store inventory. Kenco Logistics Services, one of the biggest third-party logistics companies in the nation, leased space for use as a warehouse hub. Kenco has since taken additional space to handle work for Stryker. In August 2006, Maggie's Catering moved into a 6,900-square-foot building on the

Midlink campus. Two months later, Purity Cylinder Gases moved into its new 15,000-square-foot facility. "As of the summer of 2007, the building is 50 percent occupied and we've had occupancy as high as 94 percent," said David Smith.

In February 2008, Midlink Business Park received another boost. Kaiser Aluminum, a $1.3 billion California-based manufacturer of fabricated aluminum products for aerospace, general engineering, automotive and custom industrial applications, announced that it would lease 435,000 square feet. Intending to bring 300 jobs and invest $80 million in the community, the company plans to locate an aluminum-extrusion operation at the facility. In addition to the incentives offered by the state of Michigan, Charter Township of Comstock, Kalamazoo County and the Michigan Works! Association, the caliber of the workforce and training provided by Kalamazoo Valley Community College and Western Michigan University helped Kaiser make their decision.

"Kalamazoo provides a strategic location to best serve our customers and pursue new opportunities for growth," said Jack Hockema, Chief Executive Officer of Kaiser Aluminum. The incentives offered "demonstrated that Michigan was the right place to locate and we look forward to working together toward a prosperous future."

The people who imagined and built these new facilities, with the assistance of public-private partnerships, the community and all branches of government, took what might be dubbed a *Field of Dreams* approach. They believed that if they built it, companies and people would come. Of course, this infrastructure would be useless without the people and the spirit that fills them. But the buildings were an important and necessary first step. Indeed, there's a degree to which these bricks and mortar initiatives function as the concrete foundation for Kalamazoo's Community Capitalism efforts. In order for these economic development projects to grow, to rise above the foundation and start adding stories, they will need to continue to draw on community support – be it via capital, people, government, etc. – which is vital to all building projects.

CHAPTER 4

TALENT:
TALENT GETS IT DONE

People do not decide to become extraordinary.
They decide to accomplish extraordinary things.

— SIR EDMUND HILLARY

In today's highly competitive and global market, businesses, hospitals, school systems and even entire communities need much more than bricks and mortar, or investment capital, to succeed. Everyone has access to the best technology and glossy marketing. Information and ideas are no longer proprietary. Every town in America has its main strip filled with business after business, retail shop after retail shop. So what differentiates one from the other?

Consider the question always on the typical retail shopper's mind – should I go to Kmart, Target or Wal-Mart to get what I want? Or to put the focus on Kalamazoo… Why do doctors choose to use a Triathlon knee component manufactured by Stryker as opposed to a competitor's? Why does a soccer mom choose to buy a Mercury Mountaineer over another SUV or minivan to cart her kids around? Why does an excited bride-to-be choose to have her wedding at the Radisson Plaza Hotel as opposed to another venue?

People. That's the difference. In many instances, the employees or people that work at these businesses make other people or consumers choose to patronize these companies. Whether it's a start-up with five employees or a 100-year-old company with 15,000 employees, the differentiating factor is talent. In today's world, where people have enormous choice – not just locally, but around the nation and around the globe – on where to get services ranging from construction management to accounting, it is imperative to select, not just hire, the right people.

People are not our most important asset.
The right people are.

– JIM COLLINS

It's not enough to fill an empty job. You have to fill it with the person who is uniquely qualified to carry out the responsibilities. Any able person can open a door for you as you enter a hotel, but the way in which he opens the door makes all the difference. And not everyone is wired to open a door correctly. Some people CAN open a door better than others, not because of upper-body strength, but because they can sincerely connect with each guest, have a positive and engaging smile regardless of the time of day, deliver an upbeat greeting, remember a guest's name and naturally go above and beyond to help a guest. They just can't help it – that's how they are "wired."

The companies that figure out who can open the door better are those that will be the most successful. And that involves looking beyond the printed words on the resume, beyond the letters after someone's name. "It" means getting the right people in the right position at the right time to make a company the best that it can be.

Companies need to be able to find the individuals who possess the required talents for the respective role for which they are recruiting, develop their capabilities and retain them. Once companies start finding the talented people and figure out how they did it, they attract more and more talented people. "Birds of a feather flock together," as the old proverb has it. Put another way, "Talent knows talent."

So how does a company find the right "birds?"

First, a company needs to understand what it is seeking in an employee — by studying the top performers and "calibrating its gold standard." A company looking for a research scientist may need a specific educational background and some necessary prior work experience. But beyond that, is the company looking for a great orator who talks a good game, or for an extremely detail-oriented person who doesn't make a mistake? When a firm seeks a human resource specialist, does the ideal target need a human resources degree? Or must it be someone who can interact well with others? Who makes the best entry-level salesperson: a college senior who has summer work experience selling tickets at a local movie theater or the defensive end on the football team who has never worked a day in his life but who is outgoing and never missed a practice?

Research and practice have shown that credentials don't necessarily make people successful in their jobs. Sure, an Ivy League background, an internship at Goldman Sachs or three years spent as an account executive at a prominent advertising agency look good on paper. But ultimately, natural talent is frequently a more powerful predictor of on-the-job success. So too are the intrinsic drives and motivations that inspire people to perform their core roles effectively.

HUMANeX, the company that originated the concept of a "talent-driven organization," defines what makes a person successful in their job as 50 percent "talent" and 50 percent "advantages." The 50 percent "advantages" side can be further broken up into 12.5 percent education, 12.5 percent experience and 25 percent fit. That's the easy stuff to figure out. It's the 50 percent "talent" side that is most critical and can't be acquired by reading a book or attending a class. But once it is identified, the "talent" can help companies find the right "birds."

So rather than know whether a position requires knowledge of a certain computer language, employers have to get their hands around what human attributes the position requires: responsibility, compassion, sociability, discipline, focus, ethics, empathy, competitiveness, creativity, persuasiveness, etc.

Once a company truly understands what it is looking for, it needs to reconsider its interview process. Forget the standard "Tell me about your favorite class at the University of Michigan" or "Describe your biggest challenge in increasing your revenues during the past year." Try asking some of the following:

- What are you passionate about in your work?
- On a scale of 1 to 10, with 10 being high, how would you and others that know you well, rate your level of performance against your peers?
- In your work, what are you a "pro" at?
- Define and give me an example of how you go "above and beyond" in your work.
- How are you driven to meet and exceed customer expectations?

People who are consistent top performers at certain jobs, it turns out, answer certain questions in similar ways. Once you know the answers you seek, it's easy to identify and hire the individuals who answer the questions in the right way. But hiring is only a first step. Employees need ongoing training. They need to be told when they do something well. They need to feel as if their employers care about them and reward them with increased responsibility as they prove themselves.

It all sounds easy and like common sense. But of course, it's not. And too many companies still have personnel policies that involve trying to fit square pegs into round holes. In this regard, however, Kalamazoo is unique. It figured this out long ago and is now home to the largest number of talent-driven organizations in the country.

It all started at Stryker Corporation in the mid-1980s. Ron Elenbaas was named President of the Surgical Group in 1985 and was determined to do something about the 40 percent turnover rate in his sales force, while also building a world-class workforce that would be the best in the industry. He recruited Brad Black to take over as Vice President of Human Resources in 1986. Brad Black had sharpened his approach to human resource leadership and organization development at one of the top *Good to Great* organizations identified in Jim Collins' classic management book.

Talent is the product. With the right people, given the correct incentives, encouraged and driven to their highest individual accomplishments...you will adapt to most competitive challenges. You will weather more rain delays, bad ump calls, flat beers in the concession stands and all routine disasters of the zero sum standings most organizations are facing. Talent is the product.

— JEFF ANGUS

Brad Black spent the next 10 years with Stryker building an empirical model focusing on talent and culture that separates the best from the rest. He and his group interviewed and studied the best salespersons at Stryker and figured out what made them tick. Then the company did the unthinkable. Stryker rejected its traditional means of hiring, which focused on resumes, experience and instinctive judgments based on interviews. Next, it developed an interview process that focused on talent or the way people are "wired" and fit for the role, the team and the unique culture into which they were hired.

What Stryker discovered was eye-opening. Stryker found that the best medical device salesperson was not necessarily a traditional device or health care salesperson. Rather, the person could also be someone who had traded on the floor of the Chicago Board of Trade, or who had sold air time for a television station or spent three years as a linebacker in the National Football League. Or the individual could be a banker, an Oscar Mayer hot dog salesperson, a former Secret Service Agent or even a recent college graduate with no formal sales experience at all. What really mattered was how the person was "wired."

A genius is a talented person who does his homework.

— THOMAS EDISON

As the new policies were implemented, turnover fell from 40 percent annually to less than 10 percent in two years. The performance of the sales team contributed to Stryker's trend of superior revenue and profit growth that has resulted in the company's stock over the past 25 years achieving an impressive 28 percent compound annual growth rate. "We referred to it as the offense," said Brad Black, "because we had a play-book with proven plays designed to execute a focused discipline while the rest of the world, including our competitors, was playing defense."

"Education and experience are nice, but it's not the be all and end all. Talent is the critical foundation – the natural ability not acquired through effort – for a highly successful workforce," he continued. "Talent can be better visualized or thought of as a pyramid with thought and learning style at the apex, supported by influence, then relation-ships, next work style and finally, at the foundation, a person's values and drives. And for a company, it's a matter of not just selecting talent carefully, but developing it. If that idea is hardwired into a company and their managers and leaders create a culture where people are cared about and engaged, then that company is going to be successful."

During his tenure at Stryker, Brad Black made many business contacts who became close friends. One of the unique things about Kalamazoo is that the community willingly shares best practices across industries in order to raise the level of human capital available in the region. And these leaders of various industries talk to one another a lot. One of those individuals who befriended Brad Black was Bill Johnston.

In May 2000, when Bill Johnston acquired the Radisson Plaza Hotel from the Upjohn Company and immediately set about redeveloping the property in a multimillion-dollar expansion effort, he knew that more square footage wouldn't be a key differentiator in making the Radisson successful.

"We had to totally restructure the business, form a sales team and build a new presence in downtown Kalamazoo," Bill Johnston said. The Radisson would not only renovate its structure, it would renovate its workforce. "It wouldn't happen overnight; I knew it would take three to four years," he added.

Talent is the differentiator.
Your marketing or technology can be great,
but talent is what makes you truly successful.

— BILL JOHNSTON

The Radisson began working with Brad Black to restructure the way it selects employees and to develop processes for continuous training and improvement. It also built a 9,000-square-foot training and development center and required that new employees go through 40 hours of training before they begin working with customers, as opposed to the industry standard of 4 hours. All employees undergo a talent-driven interview and are slotted into positions based upon their responses.

The numerical results have been impressive. Each year, the hotel's occupancy rate has improved and it finished 2007 with a 64 percent occupancy rate – a full five points higher than the state average. Thanks to the popularity of its restaurants, food and beverage sales generate about 65 percent of revenues. The hotel employs 680 people and each year brings 850,000 people to downtown, as guests, as diners and as conference-goers.

Bill Johnston believes that service has made a difference. The Radisson is now a four-diamond property. "The service is what really

For the fourth year in a row, Lincoln Industries, a manufacturing company that specializes in fabrication and metal finishing, was named one of 2007's "50 Best Small & Medium Companies to Work for in America" by the Society for Human Resource Management.

HOW TO MANUFACTURE ONE OF THE BEST PLACES TO WORK FOR

A player in the manufacturing industry that continually sees a decline in production and employment, Lincoln Industries continues to defy the odds. The end of 2006 marked the company's fourteenth straight year of double-digit sales percentage increase. Over the next 10 years, the company predicts to grow 15 percent annually. In January 2007, the company of 488 employees vowed to expand by 140, but that number will prove to be closer to 200 predicts company officials.

The company's culture stresses leadership and encourages innovation. It is defined by a distinct set of "beliefs and drivers." These "beliefs and drivers" have become the foundation of the company:

LINCOLN INDUSTRIES BELIEFS
- Our people and their unique individual talents are valued.
- Appropriate recognition motivates our people to be successful.
- Leaders create value.
- Innovation creates continuous improvement.
- Profitability ensures the survival of our company.
- Positive relationships build loyalty.
- Honesty is essential in all transactions.
- We create value for our customers.
- Wellness and healthy lifestyles are important to our success.

LINCOLN INDUSTRIES SUCCESS DRIVERS
- Quality in everything we do.
- Productivity improvement is a continuous process.
- On-time delivery because our customers depend on us.
- A safe working environment is our commitment to each other.
- Environmental responsibility is our commitment to our communities.
- People development because our people create our success.
- Company growth is the result of providing a superior service.
- Value-added service means doing more for our customers.

The secret to Lincoln Industries' success is not in the machines that they use in servicing such sectors as power sports, heavy duty trucking, automotive and agriculture or the metal that they use in their finishing services. Actually, it's the people who operate the machinery and perform the plating tasks that are the special ingredient in the company's success. And that's what Lincoln Industries calls its employees – people.

Lincoln Industries' hiring plan is simple: Find someone with talent and then teach them the skills they need to be successful. To that end, the company has developed their own college for training and development, the Vision College. The sole purpose of the Vision College is to develop talents to improve performance. The college provides professional skills training, development resources and services, leadership development and environmental, safety and health training. All levels of the organization are encouraged to attend.

The company's commitment to culture is shown in their bi-annual confidential internal surveys that grade the company and its leadership in such areas as communication, development and supervision. And continually scoring high doesn't seem to stop anyone from trying to improve the next go-around.

Recognition is also a big part of the picture. Quality and service achievements are recognized in their daily and monthly newsletters. Roundtables held once a month between randomly selected company members and senior management stimulate interaction and drive improvements. Monthly "Champion" programs honor quality and service accomplishments on all three shifts – not just the visible day shift. An annual banquet celebrates company accomplishments and outstanding achievers.

What Lincoln Industries has manufactured is an environment that has come to be defined by its people. They are a testament that high standards and quality do not have to be given up in order to obtain higher sales and revenues. The rest of the manufacturing industry would be well-served to take note.

drives the financials," he said. "If you don't differentiate yourself, you are outpaced. Talent is the differentiator. Your marketing or technology can be great, but talent is what makes you truly successful."

The service is noticed. "From the second you walk in the revolving door, the guy that's parking the car is friendly and on top of his game," noted Aaron Zeigler, President of the Harold Zeigler Automotive Group. "You walk into a restaurant, the service is phenomenal." And Aaron Zeigler should know. His family's eponymous auto dealership company also uses the principles of the talent-driven organization.

On a joint family vacation, Bill Johnston shared his success story with Aaron Zeigler's father, Harold Zeigler, founder of the Kalamazoo-based auto dealership company. After a few months of careful consideration, Harold Zeigler decided to adapt the concept to his organization. Harold Zeigler Automotive Group has 24 franchises in nine dealerships throughout Michigan, Indiana and Illinois. The group employs about 500 people and reports annual sales of more than $300 million.

Becoming a talent-driven organization has allowed us to be proactive instead of being reactive.

— AARON ZEIGLER

Until four years ago, Harold Zeigler Automotive Group had generally recruited employees through traditional means, using classified ads in the newspaper and word of mouth. When Harold Zeigler Automotive Group initially committed to becoming a talent-driven organization, it began profiling employees and realigning them with their talents. "For example, we profiled a person who had been in a sales position and was not too successful at it. It turned out that he needed to be in an accounting position, and he went from being not so productive to being a controller of a dealership," said Aaron Zeigler.

Profiles were created for each of the positions the automotive group had to fill. Several key employees were then selected and taught how to do structured interviews. For a salesperson, the company seeks certain personality themes: a competitive spirit, an ability to think creatively, somebody who is persuasive, focused and has high relationship skills. For a manager, the profile would be someone who is driven to lead a team, develop the department's effectiveness, efficiency and financial performance and who can help develop and retain people.

"Becoming a talent-driven organization has allowed us to be proactive instead of being reactive," said Aaron Zeigler. The auto sales industry typically suffers from extremely high turnover – 70 percent to

80 percent per year. But in 2006, Ziegler's turnover was 18 percent. "It greatly reduces our cost and allows us to focus on finding really good people, instead of having to fill holes," said Aaron Zeigler. Other metrics such as sales and customer satisfaction have risen as well. Through mid-2007, same-store sales were up 20 percent over the year before – at a time when industry sales were essentially flat.

Over time, more businesses in Kalamazoo began to learn about the advantages of talent-driven organizations. "When business people began to see the positive change, they began to inquire, 'What are you doing here?'" said Bill Johnston. Word began to spread, and Brad Black said he saw the potential for what he dubbed "a talent-driven community" – a concentration of organizations, for-profit and non-profit, public and private, who share knowledge and best practices on how to select and develop talent.

On their own, many of the presidents of the talent-driven organizations began to meet for breakfast and share knowledge. Also, every two months, at a talent-driven community event, one or two organizations highlight a best practice for recognition. It's like open-source software, an operating system that can be used at a range of companies. In addition, Brad Black teaches courses to executives at companies in fields ranging from medical devices to insurance, and yes, even economic development. "They're all in the community of learning at the same time," he said.

The strong take from the weak
but the smart take from the strong.

– PETE CARRIL

After his success at Stryker, Brad Black was recruited to The Gallup Organization in 1995 to develop new practices for the polling group to use with their clients. Starting in 2003, he served in a top leadership position with a Gallup spin-off. But at a morning breakfast meeting in early 2007, several heads of Kalamazoo-based companies convinced him to hang up his own shingle. HUMANeX, Brad Black's own baby, now has a unique focus on the talent-driven organization.

HUMANeX works to help companies place people in jobs in which they are wired to succeed and thus build a culture of success. But it has a more widespread vision. Brad Black wants to take his premise a step further and build entire communities that are talent-driven. Kalamazoo is the ideal spot to start because, as a result of widespread adoption, the city is the best living and breathing lab for the talent-driven methodology and design in America – with more than 20 companies across a range of industries using it.

"There isn't such a concentration of client partners anywhere in America, not even on Fifth Avenue in New York City," said Brad Black. "The group in Kalamazoo has proven to be an effective networking organization, since talent-driven organizations like to work with one another." He has established offices in Kalamazoo and Lincoln, Nebraska, with the goal of spreading his talent-driven network in each of those cities. His goal is then to grow into other cities across America.

Examples of companies that have adopted the methodology and have experienced tremendous success include Schupan & Sons, Inc., an aluminum and recycling company; Kalamazoo Valley Community College, whose president, Marilyn Schlack, adapted it to hire instructors and professors; and CSM Group, a construction management company. Other companies that have experienced a clear impact include Greenleaf Hospitality, Greenleaf Trust, Southwest Michigan First, Pro Services and Keyser Insurance Group. Newer organizations embracing the culture are Contractors Mechanical, GlobeFunder, The Kalamazoo Gazette and a number of local school systems.

"The analogy we use of selecting top talent is it's like getting a better pair of glasses," said CSM Group President, Steve East. Before adopting the concept of a talent-driven organization, CSM Group had focused on resumes. But it has since learned that "they don't matter anymore." CSM Group puts potential employees through a series of interviews, including what it calls a "fit interview," in which candidates meet with different members of CSM Group's team in different situations. The goal is to see if the potential employee fits in. "It's important to get the talent and fit issue down first," said Steve East. "We're looking for people to embrace our mission, vision and values. We can teach you the skills." He reported that CSM Group's retention is excellent and that revenues have grown 30 percent annually for the past three years. That's big in the highly competitive construction market.

> *The analogy we use of selecting top talent*
> *is that it's like getting a better pair of glasses.*
>
> — STEVE EAST

From Upjohn to Stryker, organizations in Kalamazoo have always thought big. Bronson Methodist Hospital, a not-for-profit, locally-owned and operated entity, was no different. "We thought we could be a national leader in health care quality," said Frank Sardone. Doing so would bring clear benefits to the hospital, its employees and, most importantly, its patients. In conjunction with their structural additions, Bronson resolved to pursue a Malcolm Baldrige National Quality Award, part of a competition established by the U.S. Commerce Department in 1987 to encourage American companies to boost competitiveness. Undergoing the process forced Bronson to re-examine the way it did business, looking at everything from the way it managed the intensive care unit to the way it trained nurses.

The hospital set a goal of winning the award by 2010. But the drive for quality began to pay dividends in relatively short order. In April 2006, Bronson received the 2005 Baldrige Award – four years ahead of schedule – and became only the sixth hospital to do so. Additionally, the hospital's mortality rate was among the lowest in the nation. Across a variety of metrics, quality improved. One of the biggest, and most gratifying, areas of improvement has been in staff focus.

At The Cheesecake Factory, top executives don't worry so much about how much cream cheese to mix into their specialty desserts; rather, they concern themselves more with the individuals who serve those delectable dishes.

It all started in the 1940s in a small basement kitchen in Detroit. Evelyn Overton, renowned for her cheesecake recipe, baked the cakes while caring for her two small children. To supplement their family income, her husband Oscar sold the cheesecakes to some of the best restaurants in town.

LET THEM EAT CAKE... CHEESECAKE THAT IS...

In 1971, their son David relocated to California and convinced his parents to move their business to Los Angeles. There, they opened a modest 700-square-foot store and Evelyn continued baking while Oscar sold to local restaurants. Los Angeles loved cheesecake too. In 1978, David joined the family business full-time and moved the operation to a 100-seat establishment in Beverly Hills. Since then, business has boomed to say the least.

From its humble inception, The Cheesecake Factory has achieved big things to correspond with its big portions. With a 19-page menu used at over 112 restaurants worldwide, the company boasts annual revenue of $1.2 billion. In 2005, net profit was $87.5 million. The Cheesecake Factory achieves sales of $1,000 per square foot at each location, more than double the average for casual dining chains. Even more amazing is that its turnover rate is 15 percent lower than the restaurant industry average. How does The Cheesecake Factory achieve such big numbers?

Company executives feel it's their consistent theme of hiring and retaining the right people. They employ a selective recruitment process in creative ways to identify the best "fit" for employees. By "fit," The Cheesecake Factory means that the company works to match employees with jobs they like to do. It feels that finding the right "fit" for someone in the organization leads to increased employee performance, happiness and retention.

When interviewing potential employees, interviewers look for natural ability and potential rather than for skill and knowledge. The company feels that skill and knowledge can be taught and are therefore not representative of someone's "talent" and potential to do a job well.

To that end, the company invests more than $2,000 per hourly employee annually on training. Servers, who make up more than 40 percent of the company's 27,000-member workforce, participate in a mandated two-week certification process before they even approach a table. After a month on the floor, they attend follow-up classes followed by bi-annual training and an annual recertification test. During training, each server is paired with an on-the-job mentor to help reinforce company material through coaching, games and role-playing.

Even dishwashers, often the most highly turned over position in the restaurant industry, are not ignored. Recently, the company has put in place an interactive English as a Second Language program designed by LeapFrog. Though the program costs about $325 per person, The Cheesecake Factory hopes it will increase the dishwashers' ability to interact with other employees behind the scenes.

So eat cake. And when you go to The Cheesecake Factory, you get a lot of it...and excellent service along with it.

Bronson's efforts to improve the environment for its employees – by offering flexibility, a full range of benefits and concierge services – has led to listings on national best employer lists published by *Fortune* and *Working Mother*.

Rising quality acts as a form of advertising. Since 2000, patient volume has risen by 43 percent. And today, over 40 percent of Bronson's patients come from outside Kalamazoo. As a result, Bronson's quality improvements have resulted in an increase in business activity for downtown Kalamazoo. In addition, the third-party endorsements from publications like *Fortune* and *Working Mother* give Bronson a competitive advantage in recruitment and retention – which is significant for a company that employs over 4,000 highly trained people. "We have very low nursing turnover and that saves us a lot of money," said Frank Sardone. "Every time we don't have to replace a nurse, we're saving $100,000 to $150,000."

And just as the members of the talent-driven community share their best practices, Bronson decided to share its experience with the broader community. "We started a series of public education open houses to educate others about how to become a Baldrige business and industry," said Frank Sardone. "And we stepped up our offer to the community, to have everybody and anybody who wanted to learn from our experience." In total, some 18,000 people attended a series of public events. The initiative was not a public relations exercise. "The Baldrige competition gives you a framework on how to most effectively run a business," he said, "and we want the broader Kalamazoo community to benefit."

As the city's largest employer, Bronson plays a significant role in the community. And its achievement of winning the Baldrige award, which came just as Pfizer was making the decision to downsize its operations in Kalamazoo, made a wider impact. It made the community recognize that greatness is not rooted in one thing – i.e. fields of celery, paper mills, a pharmaceutical giant, etc. Kalamazoo has historically offered something exceptional to the world – something that is worthy of example. And historically, if something happens to make that something go away in Kalamazoo – another something has always replaced it. That is a true testament of the quality of the community.

Another successful approach used in Kalamazoo was to create a "pool" that talent could "jump" into and then "swim" around in together. In this case, the "pool" was the Southwest Michigan Innovation Center. Completed in 2003 in an effort to keep scientists employed by Pfizer from relocating to other parts of the country when Pfizer's downsizing was announced, the facility was intended to provide space and an opportunity for great minds to come into their own.

The Baldridge competition gives you a framework on how to most effectively run a business and we want the broader Kalamazoo community to benefit.

— FRANK SARDONE

And they did. Fourteen start-up companies were formed and used the offices, wet-lab space and state-of-the-art equipment available to them in the 58,000-square-foot incubator/accelerator. At last count, 26 companies had been started in the Southwest Michigan Innovation

Center, the Michigan Technical Education Center and in other locations throughout the community.

Clark Smith, Chief Executive Officer of Proteos, a company specializing in protein expression, said, "You've got a lot of advantages here. You have people who want you to actually grow a business in this area which is a very important thing to have and which was one of the big draws for us. In fact, it was *the draw*. Southwest Michigan made it so attractive to do that we would have felt ashamed not to take a chance and grow a business here."

A funny thing happens when you take the time to educate your employees, pay them well and treat them as equals. You end up with extremely motivated and enthusiastic people.

— KIP TINDELL

The companies have shared not only their space but their ideas; the synergy of talent has fed off of each other. Jay Goodwin, Chief Executive Officer of ADMETRx which aids drug discovery through novel data integration and preclinical profiling methodologies, credits his company's success with having "access to that sort of community of scholars and experienced people to work with and learn from."

Chris Schauer, President of PharmOptima, a preclinical research and discovery company that provides consulting and laboratory services with a goal of discovering antibiotic treatments for infectious disease, attributes his company's success to that same synergy. He noted, "We've been able to grow just because of some tremendous opportunities, tremendous collaboration and support from the community." PharmOptima grew from 10 employees in 2003 to 35 by the end of 2007. Both PharmOptima and Proteos have been named one of "Michigan's 50 Companies to Watch" by the Edward Lowe Foundation.

Okay. You are a substance abuser, ex-convict, gang member or homeless person living in the state of California. If you are poor, you oftentimes find yourself incarcerated in a state prison such as San Quentin. If you're rich, your options include residential rehabilitation facilities, such as Promises, which offers an unparalleled recovery experience. Either way, you habitually find yourself a repeat visitor at either location – on one hand at the expense of the taxpayer, on the other hand, footing the very expensive tab yourself. Or there's another option.

THREE SIMPLE RULES

Located in San Francisco's Embarcadero waterfront area is the Delancey Street Foundation. This full block of Mediterranean-style stucco and tile buildings constructed in a triangular configuration offers a different alternative. Delancey Street is the country's leading residential self-help organization for hard-core drug and alcohol addicts, ex-convicts, functionally illiterate and unskilled individuals coming from a history of personal violence and poverty. Residence is optional and obtained by simply writing a letter and then passing through an interview process that's only requirement is truthfulness.

The Delancey Street Foundation was started in 1971 by social entrepreneur Mimi Silbert with four residents in a San Francisco apartment and a $1,000 loan. The organization now encompasses six locations throughout the United States – San Francisco, California; San Juan Pueblo, New Mexico; Brewster, New York; Greensboro, North Carolina; Los Angeles, California and Stockbridge, Massachusetts – with 1,000 current residents. Throughout the years, over 14,000 people have "graduated" from the program and have led independent lives. Over 10,000 illiterate people have earned high school equivalency degrees. Over 1,000 have received a diploma from a state accredited post-secondary vocational three-year program. Over 1,000 gang members have turned away from their posse to non-violence. Residents have built or remodeled over 1,500 low-income housing units. Graduates have gone on to be account executives, business owners, lawyers, ambulance medical technicians, police officers, real estate brokers, husbands, wives, parents and so on.

The organization's staff consists of one, again Mimi Silbert, Ph.D., who serves as the program's President and Chief Executive Officer. Recognized as a national expert in criminal justice, Mimi Silbert graduated from the University of Massachusetts in 1963 and with a Masters (1965) and Doctorate (1968) in Counseling Psychology and Criminology from the University of California at Berkeley. She has received countless awards, been featured on numerous prime-time television shows and in several periodicals and received nine honorary doctorate degrees. As for the other positions in the organizations, residents fill them all. No one, incidentally, gets paid.

To keep the organization going, it costs an average of $10,000 per resident per year to run Delancey Street with an annual outlay of $4.5 million. Add to that the $30 million capital investment in the Embarcadero complex – which includes almost 200 townhouses, parks, a town hall, a movie theater, small businesses, a café bookstore and art gallery and a restaurant. Yet the foundation runs at no cost to the resident or the taxpayer. All revenue is generated by more than 20 businesses run solely by the residents.

To become a resident, one must commit two years to the organiza- tion, although one may leave at any time. The doors are never locked. The average stay is three to four years. Newcomers start at the bottom, living in dorm-like rooms with several others and performing simple maintenance duties such as sweeping, serving meals or garbage detail. In the beginning, residents can only write to their family. After that, letters, phone calls and visits must be earned. Men must trim their hair short and become clean-shaven; women must remove make-up and clothing is provided. Residents learn to develop new self images.

The organization asks its residents to obey three simple rules: No physical violence. No threats of violence. No drugs or alcohol.

Punishment for disobeying any of these three rules is cause for imme- diate removal. And it seems to work. Former gang members who swore to kill each other room together at Delancey Street. Armed robbers promote the atmosphere of non-violence in Silbert's maxim of "each one teach one." Drug dealers who never made it past seventh grade teach other drop-outs how to read. A former skinhead can even be seen helping a former African-American prostitute keep on top of her orders in the organization's restaurant.

Residents are changing their world by changing themselves. This is done by gaining an education and obtaining at least a high school equivalency degree, acquiring three marketable skills – one manual skill, one clerical/computer skill and one interpersonal/sales skill – and learning the life skills of accountability, responsibility, dignity, decency and integrity. All this is done on the premises by working in one of Delancey Street's training schools. Vocational programs offered include accounting and bookkeeping, automotive repair, moving and trucking, Christmas tree sales, film screening, construction and property management, restaurant services and digital printing.

These vocational programs are not "Mickey Mouse" operations by any means. The Delancey Street Restaurant at Embarcadero is a four-star establishment. Those involved in construction actually build Delancey Street's residences, most notably being the Embarcadero location which was built at half of its assessed cost. The automotive shop services over 100 vehicles at any given time and has refurbished eight antique cars, including a 1916 Willys Overland Convertible and a 1930 General Motors double-decker bus. The San Francisco screening room is written up as one of the top three in that city.

So Delancey Street offers a different solution to solve the social ills of the world. They don't try to change the past; rather they try to change the future. Mistakes can be made, but they must be admitted to and fixed. People are taught to focus on their strengths, not their problems. Everyone is a giver and everyone is a receiver. Following three simple rules can indeed make the world a better place.

Of the 26 companies started, four have outgrown their space and moved out of the Southwest Michigan Innovation Center. And the spaces they vacated have already been filled by new ventures.

One of the companies that "graduated" from the Innovation Center is Kalexsyn, a medicinal chemistry contract research firm engaged in the drug discovery process. Kalexsyn was started by two scientists, David Zimmermann and Robert Gadwood, with a "great idea" and has since grown to 23 employees. On October 16, 2007, as Kalexsyn with Governor Jennifer Granholm's aid cut the ribbon on their new facility, David Zimmermann, Chief Executive Officer of Kalexsyn, said, "We are most certainly celebrating our company's strategic growth. But we are also celebrating reinvestment in southwest Michigan. We are celebrating the success of public-private partnerships."

Successful human capital programs can prove the difference between failure and growth, which is one reason many organizations keep their secrets closely held. But by sharing best practices and knowledge, whether it is through a community of talent-driven organizations, through a message of quality or a pooling of talent, Kalamazoo has taken steps to raise the level of human capital across the entire region.

By doing so, companies – whether they are Fortune 500 firms or start-ups – can make the best possible use of the region's most significant natural resource – its people.

Indeed, putting the right people in the right place at the right time allows many of the Kalamazoo region's businesses and organizations to provide exceptional customer service and to be exceptional themselves.

CHAPTER 5

EDUCATION:
THE PROMISE OF A BRIGHTER FUTURE

Education is not filling a bucket but lighting a fire.

— WILLIAM B. YEATS

A revitalized downtown, availability of capital, new physical infrastructures and investment in talent-driven organizations are all important components of the Community Capitalism strategy. But any gains realized from such efforts would be temporary, if at all, if a community doesn't attract and retain a population base that wants to learn, work and build businesses.

Public schools play an enormously important role in this dynamic. After all, school performance has incredibly powerful economic knock-on effects, from creating a skilled local workforce to building property values. A highly rated public school system attracts residents to a town like bears to honey. A poorly performing school system serves as a centrifugal force that sends people packing.

In Kalamazoo, as is the case in many communities, the schools had become a challenge in recent years. Due to job loss and demographic shifts, the student body of its schools was shrinking consistently. In 2005, the school district of about 10,000 students – comprised of a majority of minority students (about 50 percent African-American and 8 percent Hispanic) – was somewhat bifurcated. While an exceptional math and science center, the Kalamazoo Area Mathematics and Science Center, provided advanced courses for college-bound students, graduation rates based on the cumulative promotion index for minorities were, at the end of the 2004-2005 school year, 43.1 percent – with just 467 students graduating.

There was a sense in the community that dramatic efforts were needed to reverse potential decline. If Kalamazoo was to continue down this erosion of the middle class within the school system, there would be two sets of populations. There would be the students that were in the honors program, those at the bottom and very little in between.

The solution? In a place where capital had been created to attract business, why not create the equivalent of a venture capital fund that would invest in the city's youngest, and perhaps, most valuable human capital – its children? Doing so would send a message to families in Kalamazoo and throughout the nation – that Kalamazoo students face a bright future.

The Kalamazoo Promise is... 'an imaginative new approach to economic development.'
– THE ECONOMIST

Early in 2005, school officials were already busy working on making improvements, starting with the quality of education. Janice Brown, who was named Superintendent of the Kalamazoo Public School System in 2000, was leading an effort to adapt the mindset of continuous improvement in the schools, tracking the efforts that Bronson Methodist Hospital had been making. "We developed a vision that we would educate every child, at every opportunity, every time," she said. The effort was to start by focusing on literacy at the K-3 level.

The efforts would receive a massive boost in the fall of 2005. For several years, Janice Brown and community leaders had been engaged in conversations about what it would take to revitalize Kalamazoo – economically and psychologically. "It became clear to me, after many of my biased focuses on education, education, education, that it's not education; it's economics," Janice Brown said. "When education is viewed as the key and the hope of the future, economically and aesthetically, there's great hope for the entire community."

So the discussions began to focus on a series of questions. What would draw people back to Kalamazoo? What would create economic vitality? What would bring positive attention and focus to the community?

Developments like the Southwest Michigan Innovation Center and the Southwest Michigan First Life Science Fund were surely helping. But their impact would pale in comparison to a dramatic effort, discussed behind closed doors, to shape the environment: the promise of a college education to any student who graduated from Kalamazoo public schools.

The impulse behind what is now known as the Kalamazoo Promise was certainly philanthropic. But, at its root, it was an economic development initiative. With college costs rising inexorably, the anonymous benefactors behind the program realized that the promise of full college scholarships would create enormous incentives – for children in the Kalamazoo school system to graduate and go on to college; for parents and families to get involved with their students and with the schools themselves; for people to stay in Kalamazoo; and for people all over the country – and the world – to bring their hopes and dreams with them to southwest Michigan.

In September 2005, a group of anonymous donors decided to make the graduating class of 2006 the first class eligible for the Kalamazoo Promise. And so on Thursday, November 10, 2005, an ordinary Kalamazoo School Board meeting ended up being extraordinary. Janice Brown stepped to the podium and announced the remarkable gift to

The Republic of South Africa is the country at the southern tip of Africa that borders the Atlantic and Indian Oceans. Centuries ago, the area, then known as the Cape of Good Hope, was circumnavigated by European explorers in search of the riches of India. Portuguese fishing settlements first popped up along the coast, but were later replaced by a Dutch presence that began with the establishment of a provisioning station by the Dutch East India Company in 1652. The expanding Dutch settlement gradually produced labor shortages that were solved by the enslavement of the native population.

YOU CAN'T BUILD A NEW HOUSE WITHOUT A FOUNDATION

When the Dutch East India Company declared bankruptcy, the British annexed the Cape Colony in 1806. With the discovery of diamonds in 1867 and gold in 1886, not only did the economy, immigration and the subjugation of the natives grow, but so did the tension between the English and the Boers, Dutch farmers who had moved out of the Cape Colony into neighboring areas. After a series of wars ended between the two groups, the British maintained sovereignty over the South African republics in exchange for assuming the Boer war debt and denying "blacks" the vote in all republics except the Cape Colony.

When the National Party was elected to power in 1948, it began implementing apartheid – the legal segregation of peoples into groups based upon race. While the white minority enjoyed a standard of living comparable to that of the most wealthy nations in the world, the black majority remained hindered in all levels of society – income, education, housing, medical care and life expectancy.

In 1990 after worldwide sanctions and divestments were imposed on the country and unrest within grew to stratospheric proportions, the National Party lifted its ban on the African National Congress, released Nelson Mandela from prison and gradually began removing its apartheid legislation.

Despite the end of apartheid, millions of South Africans, mostly black, continue to live in poverty. This is partly attributed to the legacy of the apartheid system, the failure of the current government to tackle social issues, the inability of that same government to spur economic growth and deal with wealth redistribution and the rampant AIDS pandemic.

So how does one turn this around? By tackling one issue at a time – or building one house at a time rather than a whole city. And in order to do this, a solid foundation must be laid first.

Oprah Winfrey sees such a foundation in girls' education. And she's doing something about it. On January 2, 2007, the world's only female African-American billionaire opened the Oprah Winfrey Leadership Academy for Girls in the small town of Henley-on-Klip, south of Johannesburg in South Africa.

This $40 million academy is currently giving over 150 girls from deprived backgrounds a quality education when they probably otherwise would have had none. The academy hopes to grow their student population to 450. Girls are selected for attendance based upon academic and leadership potential and must be from a home where the monthly income is less than $787.

Oprah Winfrey's motives are unselfish. Out of her respect for Nelson Mandela and her desire to embrace her own African roots, Oprah Winfrey hopes to make a change in the African nation through girls' education. The benefits could be astronomical. If young girls are surrounded by inspirational facilities and instructors, she believes the potential of the girls to become successful and inspirational themselves and exponentially bring change to others will come to fruition. Also, studies have shown that educated girls are less likely to get HIV/AIDS and this is an important factor in a country where a 2006 South African Department of Health Study projected that 29.1 percent of pregnant women were living with HIV and 13.6 percent of teenage girls were afflicted.

Centuries ago, the thought of an African-American woman someday working to correct the ramifications of the explorations of European navigators would never have crossed the minds of explorers like Bartolomeu Dias as they sailed around the Cape of Good Hope on their East Indies' trade routes.

the community. Tears flowed, shouts of joy were heard and the feelings around the room could only be described as rapturous and blessed.

The announcement was shocking – in a good way. "Board members were crying, audience members were crying," recalled Janice Brown. Within days, every major news network had picked up the story, which was covered by media outlets as far away as Australia. To this day, the Kalamazoo Promise garners attention. As recently as February 2007, Katie Couric of the CBS Evening News visited Kalamazoo Central High School as one of her segments on "The American Spirit," which profiles remarkable people tackling big problems.

While one might guess that it must be complicated, the Kalamazoo Promise is a deceptively simple program designed to reward residence and enrollment in the Kalamazoo Public School District. For students who have lived in the Kalamazoo Public School District for at least four years, upon graduation, the program will pay 65 percent of tuition and fees at any public university or community college in the state of Michigan. The proportion of fees paid rises with length of attendance, to the point where those who started school in Kalamazoo in kindergarten receive full scholarships upon graduating from high school.

> *Let us think of education as the means of developing our greatest abilities, because in each of us there is a private hope and dream which, fulfilled, can be translated into benefit for everyone and greater strength for our nation.*
>
> — JOHN F. KENNEDY

The Kalamazoo Promise, a 501(c)(3) organization, has one employee, administrator Bob Jorth. Seniors fill out two one-page forms in the fall and provide the Kalamazoo Promise with three schools in which they are interested. The students must apply to the schools on their own and the Kalamazoo Promise shares their commitment with schools so students can be recruited. When students enroll in school, whether it is Kalamazoo Valley Community College or the University of Michigan, the Kalamazoo Promise pays the tuition directly to the school. Receiving funds from the Kalamazoo Promise does not disqualify students from receiving financial aid such as Pell Grants. To continue receiving funds throughout their post-secondary education, students must maintain a 2.0 grade point average or higher and maintain a minimum of 12 credit hours per semester. The estimated cost to the benevolent donors was between $2 million and $3 million the first year and projected to rise ultimately to between $10 million and $12 million annually once four classes are up and running.

In its short lifespan, the Kalamazoo Promise has proven to be a remarkable case study in the impact of positive economic incentives. In 2007, the graduation rate based on the cumulative promotion index rose sharply to 57.4 percent, with 567 students graduating. Based on figures provided by the W.E. Upjohn Institute, 404 graduates of the Kalamazoo Public School Class of 2007 took advantage of the Kalamazoo Promise to attend 17 different Michigan public universities or colleges, up from 337 graduates in 2006 attending 14 schools. About two thirds stayed local, either at Western Michigan University or Kalamazoo Valley Community College.

The largest group of students taking advantage of the Kalamazoo Promise was Kalamazoo's African-American student population. The promise of free tuition instantly encouraged students to set their aspirations higher, as the number of Kalamazoo students applying to the state's top two universities – the University of Michigan and Michigan State – more than doubled. Based on that same W.E. Upjohn Institute study, 17 students in the Class of 2006 attended the University of Michigan; in the fall of 2007, 33 Kalamazoo graduates matriculated in Ann Arbor. In the fall of 2006, 37 students entered Michigan State University; in 2007, the number rose to 52.

If you think education is expensive, try ignorance.

– DEREK BOK

The Kalamazoo Promise has clearly provided a spur to students to graduate, but it has also changed the long-term thinking of people in Kalamazoo – and beyond. In the past two years, as virtually every surrounding district in southwest Michigan lost students, Kalamazoo gained students. Enrollment rose by 986 in the fall of 2006, to 11,203,

In 1973, the Carpenters' lyrics, "Sing, sing a song; sing out loud; sing out strong; sing of good things not bad; sing of happy not sad," were the rage. In a country like Rwanda, one would think that no one would be singing, let alone be singing of good things. Yet some are...

SING, SING A SONG...

A young child in Rwanda has a high potential of being an orphan. With a life expectancy rate of 48.99 years, a birthright into war against Hutu extremist insurgents, a 60 percent likelihood of living below the poverty line and a high degree of risk of contracting an infectious disease such as malaria, adults do not have a good chance of making it to their child's first day of pre-school let alone their wedding.

As a result, many Rwandan children find themselves alone in the world and in orphanages. Due to the large population of orphans, orphanages do not have the ability to provide even a portion of a child's daily basic needs, things we take for granted like food, shelter and a change of clothes.

Step in the African Children's Choir. The African Children's Choir strives to raise awareness of the plight of African orphans and to raise funds to be used for the group's relief and development programs. The group is currently providing support for over 6,700 children in the countries of Uganda, Sudan, Kenya, Rwanda, Nigeria, Ghana and South Africa.

For example, in Uganda, the group's original area of operation in Africa, funds have helped to support the African Children's Choir Academy, which readies children for concert tours; two literacy schools in Kampala; a nursery school in the village of Luwero; a primary school called the African Outreach Academy; the Agricultural Farm School, which provides produce to their schools and local markets; and various secondary and trade schools throughout the country.

For the past 21 years, the African Children's Choir, comprised of African children ages 7 through 11 who are musical and have lost one or both parents to the hardships of the African continent, has performed throughout North America and the United Kingdom. Songs performed by the group range from African – such as Apataka, Kamuwe Ekirabo and Ndyahimbisa – to Anglo – such as "Shine Jesus Shine," "How Good It Is" and "Lean On Me."

Once the children have completed the year's tour, they return to their homelands and share with their community the funds that they helped to raise for food, clothes and a Christian primary, secondary and post-secondary education that the communities could otherwise not afford.

Their story has become a circle of giving. When the children perform, they freely give their stories and musical gifts to their audience, who in turn give their monetary support to the African Children's Choir, which in turn gives the funds back to the poverty-stricken areas that these children come from. What a story.

up about 10 percent from 2005 – double what planners had expected. The increase was driven by a dramatic rise in the number of people putting down roots in Kalamazoo. People have come from 88 communities in Michigan, from 32 states and 9 foreign countries. "We think there are as many as 400 new families that have come to Kalamazoo since the announcement," said Bob Jorth. In the fall of 2007, the unaudited full-time equivalent headcount for the Kalamazoo Public School District was 11,394. That's up slightly from 2006, in a region where most outlying areas experienced decline.

The influx – and the optimism about the future – has stimulated a broader economic impact. "We're seeing families buying homes instead of renting, and adding on instead of moving," said Bob Jorth. Home values in Kalamazoo rose 6 percent in 2006, a period in which home values in the region were generally flat and the state as a whole saw a significant decline.

Meanwhile, the growth in the student population has created jobs and new economic activity on its own. Michigan's school funding scheme is conducted on a per pupil basis – so 1,000 more students at about $7,500 per student added about $7.5 million annually in funding for Kalamazoo's public schools. That has allowed the district to hire 45 new teachers. In May 2006, in anticipation of further growth, the community passed an $85 million bond issue to construct a new elementary school and a new middle school – the first new schools built in Kalamazoo in nearly 40 years. The construction of these schools will ultimately stimulate further job creation.

Within 24 months, the funds committed by the Kalamazoo Promise were clearly more than repaid in rising home values, new jobs and construction spending. More significantly, the investment yielded a tremendous return that can be measured in the more amorphous, yet crucially vital, metrics of ambition and hope. School events are attracting more parents. At one Kalamazoo public school alone, parental involvement in conferences rose 44 percent. The Kalamazoo Promise has prodded Kalamazoo's school system to make its curriculum more rigorous. In the 1800s, Kalamazoo was the first system in the state of Michigan that financed primary and secondary education with tax dollars, and it was the first in the state to have kindergarten. The Kalamazoo Promise has made Kalamazoo the state's first K-16 system.

The Kalamazoo Promise has been a remarkable and unexpected gift, and, to a degree, a challenge that the community has willingly shouldered. "If you dangle college out there without some serious consideration to preparation, it won't work for kids that are underprepared," said Janice Brown. And so it has provided an impetus to focus on all the issues that affect children's preparedness, from housing to dental care, from mentoring to tutoring.

The best way to predict your future is to create it.

— STEVEN R. COVEY

The whole notion of the Kalamazoo Promise is to force people to make a decision: Do I want to stay here and be a part of the solution, roll up my shirt sleeves and volunteer, attend conferences? Or am I willing to pass up a huge economic benefit and turn my back on it and walk away? Thus far, the answer has been overwhelmingly that people want to stick around and work for a brighter future.

Getting school children to think about college is a huge effort. But for a community concerned about retaining human capital, it's only part of the battle. Communities like Kalamazoo face a challenge in retaining local students who go away to college, as well as the thousands of students who attend local universities but pursue careers elsewhere – in Chicago, St. Louis, New York or Los Angeles. The ability to retain graduates is crucial for existing and growing companies. A second new scholarship program available to Kalamazoo-area students, the Monroe-Brown Internship Program, is attempting to address this issue.

The greatest danger for most of us is not that we aim too high and we miss it, but we aim to low and reach it.

— MICHELANGELO

Since its founding in 1986, the Kalamazoo-based Monroe-Brown Foundation has supported scholarships at the University of Michigan, Kalamazoo College and Kalamazoo Valley Community College; earmarked scholarships for top high school students from southwest Michigan; provided funds to expand the facilities and programs at the Kalamazoo Area Math and Science Center; and started a program for top high school students in Kalamazoo County to honor their favorite teachers. While these programs have all been gratifying, noted Bob Brown, "they didn't work very well in terms of motivating students to stay in Kalamazoo after graduation."

In partnership with Southwest Michigan First, the Monroe-Brown Foundation started a combined internship and scholarship program that hooked students at local colleges up with local companies while they were still in school, at a time when they are thinking seriously about where to begin their professions. The Monroe-Brown Internship Program scholarships, first offered in January 2007, are open to incoming juniors, seniors and graduate students at Western Michigan University and Kalamazoo College and students going into their second year at Kalamazoo Valley Community College. Students are required to

When we are little, we are taught being a "copy cat" is bad. As an adult, we come to realize that being a "copy cat" isn't necessarily always a bad thing. Sometimes when we copy something really good, it's a good thing.

COPY CATS

When the Kalamazoo Promise was announced in November 2005, the reaction to the announcement was in inverse proportion to its delivery. At an ordinary Kalamazoo Board of Education meeting, Kalamazoo Public Schools' Superintendent Janice Brown made a not-so-ordinary announcement. A group of anonymous donors had pledged an endowment estimated between $200 and $250 million to pay up to 100 percent of tuition to any of Michigan's state colleges or universities for graduates of Kalamazoo's public high schools.

The requirements were simple. Students must be residents within the Kalamazoo School District and attend a Kalamazoo public high school. The amount of the benefit received per individual would be between 65 percent and 100 percent of tuition based upon the individual's length of attendance in the Kalamazoo school system.

The public and media response was extraordinary. It seemed that within hours, the entire nation had heard of Kalamazoo and the Kalamazoo Promise. And not only did other communities want to learn all the details, some were willing to do the same for themselves.

Take in point some of the following copy cat "promises." While their funding sources and eligibility requirements may differ, the programs all have the same goal in mind – providing higher education to those who may not have had the opportunity otherwise,

Sponsored by Murphy Oil Corporation, the El Dorado Promise provides graduates of El Dorado High School in El Dorado, Arkansas a tuition scholarship that can be used at any accredited Arkansas public university, Arkansas community college or any accredited private or out-of-state university. Murphy Oil Corporation intended the $50 million gift to help this blue-collar city, just north of the Louisiana border, in the wake of population decline from the loss of manufacturing jobs, statewide political clout and federal funding. The El Dorado Promise provides up to five years of tuition and mandatory fees at eligible institutions.

The Oklahoma Legislature passed state legislation funding Oklahoma's Promise, the Oklahoma Higher Learning Access Program, to help resident students with a family income of less than $50,000 who maintain a 2.5 high school GPA and take a required set of college-preparatory courses. More interestingly, another requirement is that students stay away from gang involvement, drugs and alcohol. Free tuition is then granted at Oklahoma public institutions and partial tuition is available at Oklahoma private schools.

A combination of local sales and school taxes and private donations help to fund the Newton Promise in Iowa. This quaint Midwestern town hopes its promise will gain it national notoriety as a great place to raise a family and start, expand or locate a business. The Newton Promise grants up to a 100 percent tuition scholarship to graduates of Newton High School to any public state of Iowa university or community college or an equivalent amount for use at a private college in Iowa.

Tax revenues from riverboat gambling provide the basis for funding for the College Bound Scholarship Program in Hammond, Indiana. Also based on a percentage scale, College Bound requires home ownership within the school district and eligible students' parents or guardians must remain residents and home owners during college attendance. Qualified high school graduates in the City of Hammond have access to $7,500 per year at any Indiana-accredited college or university. The program is designed to increase home ownership, which the city hopes will in turn improve community education and stability.

So whether the source of money is a mystery (anonymous donors in Kalamazoo), black gold (oil money in El Dorado) or the Lucky 7s (riverboat slot machines in Hammond), the college tuition program "promises" around the country are all a good thing.

Even if they are copy cats...

work 400 hours at paid internships at local companies between April and September. Upon completing the internship, students receive a $500 bonus from both the Monroe-Brown Foundation and from their employer. In addition, the Monroe-Brown Foundation provides two payments of $2,500 at the end of each of the two successfully completed semesters after the internship. The total value is $6,000, plus 400 hours' wages at the hourly rate offered by the sponsoring companies.

In February 2007, 512 applicants applied for the positions offered at local companies. In April 2007, the selected students began their internships. Ryan Long, a 25-year-old native of southwest Michigan who had worked as a trim carpenter and property manager for several years before enrolling at Western Michigan University to study engineering, was one of the selected interns. A Monroe-Brown Internship Program intern at CSM Group, the construction management firm, he worked as a project engineer on an assignment for the Marshall, Michigan public schools. "The experience correlated with what I was learning in my civil engineering classes," said Ryan Long. "And it allowed me to know wholeheartedly that this is what I want to do when I graduate. I am not looking for a job. I am looking for a career." The wages he earned, coupled with the scholarship, allowed him to graduate without needing to take further loans. In turn, the internship helped him understand that he is heading down the right career path.

I am not looking for a job. I am looking for a career.

― RYAN LONG

Ryan Long was one of two Monroe-Brown Internship Program interns at CSM Group, where about one-third of the staff are graduates of Western Michigan University. "It is meant to keep the best and brightest in our community," said Steve East. The internships give students a sense of the length to which their careers can go in southwest Michigan. "Somebody once asked me what an intern can anticipate at CSM Group," he recalled. "And I realized that 20 years ago, I hired two kids out of Western as interns, and now they are vice presidents. I guess that's what you can anticipate."

Companies have also reaped immediate benefits by tapping into new sources of talent. Landscape Forms, the 220-employee firm based in Kalamazoo that makes high-end outdoor furniture, had three Monroe-Brown Internship Program interns this summer. "The nice thing about the Monroe-Brown Internship Program is that it's based on the assets of the community. It's something that we can plug into with a minimum of effort," said Bill Main, Chief Executive Officer of Landscape Forms. The company has a constant need for engineering and technical staff to support its design and product development and was lucky enough to have one of its three interns "very adept at a specific CAD application that we are adding to our website which will improve our marketing."

Southwest Michigan First also experienced reciprocal benefits with its intern, Mary Kate Compton. In her final year at Kalamazoo Valley Community College, she is pursuing a degree as a microcomputer technician. Mary Kate Compton shared her technical computer skills with the Southwest Michigan First staff in exchange for being exposed to the economic development environment. The experience also helped broaden her people and research skills. "I've read about things that I never would have otherwise," she reflected at the end of her internship. "I thought I would be helping people by fixing their computers as my father does, but because of the business environment that exists around Southwest Michigan First, I'm now looking at that kind of career as well."

In the future, Bob Brown envisions even further growth in the program and building an interactive website where employers and students can keep in touch, "so that if they go to Los Angeles or Chicago for a few years, they can come back."

The Monroe-Brown Internship Program is meant to keep the best and brightest in our community.

— STEVE EAST

Of course, both the Kalamazoo Promise and the Monroe-Brown Internship Program, required substantial capital. And even more importantly, they required a substantial commitment from community members who had the foresight to recognize that the amount of funds invested in these programs is secondary. These initiatives are about leadership, vision, sending a message and creating a positive image for a community. Programs like the Kalamazoo Promise created, and continue to generate, an enormous amount of buzz, excitement and interest. Kalamazoo community leaders note that at least 100 communities around the country have reached out to learn about how they can create their own versions of the Kalamazoo Promise. But it is important to note that successful replication of the Kalamazoo Promise has more to do with will than with philanthropy, resources and structure; it has to do with commitment and belief in one's community.

At its inception, the Kalamazoo Promise was an attempt to improve the quality of life for all residents – present and future – of the city. And it is clearly producing results as seen in rising home prices, new home construction, a rising school population and growing community pride. This public-private partnership – the promise of funds from private sources along with the promise of higher performance by the Kalamazoo public schools – has served as a highly effective urban revitalization program, attracting people and investment to Kalamazoo's city limits. The addition of the Monroe-Brown Internship Program to the mix has addressed the city's need to get college graduates to remain in Kalamazoo after graduation to increase the available talent pool of potential employees.

Together, both programs have certainly made Kalamazoo's future not only brighter, but promising.

CONCLUSION:
THE PIECES OF THE PUZZLE

The attention economy is a star system ...
If there is nothing very special about your work,
no matter how hard you apply yourself
you won't get noticed, and that increasingly means
you won't get paid much either.

— MICHAEL GOLDHABER

With perspective that sometimes only the passage of time can bring, Southwest Michigan First can offer the following "lessons learned" as the region has built its Community Capitalism model.

When Pfizer announced its lay-offs in 2003, the Southwest Michigan Innovation Center was ready to open. Rather than the announcement being another devastating blow to the economy and the community helpless to do anything about it, displaced workers had the wet labs and office space they needed to get their feet back on the ground and remain in Kalamazoo. Thinking ahead and being proactive rather than reactive, paid off in spades for Kalamazoo – and it can for many other communities, too.

By taking the ultimate "build it and they will come" leap of faith to invest in the speculative incubator without even a single lease commitment, Kalamazoo was able to retain its valuable scientific talent and avert the "brain drain" that so many other communities experience in the same situation. Bold initiatives rather than band-aid solutions are often what it takes to survive in today's ultra-competitive environment.

> *There are risks and costs to a program of action,*
> *but they are far less than the longer range*
> *risks and costs of comfortable inaction.*
>
> – JOHN F. KENNEDY

Southwest Michigan First could not have accomplished what it did on its own. For example, the Kalamazoo Promise was made possible by the beneficence of anonymous donors with faith in the city's future. To take the Kalamazoo Promise one step further, the economic development organization partnered with a local foundation dedicated to furthering higher education to launch the Monroe-Brown Internship Program. Almost every community or region has pockets of wealth or organizations that can be tapped into for the greater good. Be creative about finding partners.

No doubt about it: money talks. The Southwest Michigan First Life Science Fund has attracted companies to Kalamazoo that would have otherwise gone elsewhere. It may be difficult for some communities to raise $50 million in private capital, but a much smaller seed fund will pay good dividends for a region's future if invested wisely in companies with good growth potential.

Capital can and does go anywhere in this world. Individuals, institutions and companies have the ability – even the responsibility – to diversify and to invest funds anywhere around the globe. A healthy retirement account should contain domestic and international stocks, bonds *and* real estate. And there's a degree to which capital has a mind of its own, drawn by magnetic force to the next hot area or industry, wherever that may lie. But as the Kalamazoo experience has shown, there are also powerful countervailing forces that combat the centrifugal force of globalization. These include the attraction of home, the connection to a community, the loyalty to an area that has produced wealth and the desire to ensure a future of continuity and prosperity. In many instances, companies, individuals and institutions find it both attractive and necessary to invest close to home and to lend a hand to neighbors. This ability and desire to be both a citizen of the world, a global traveler concerned with big-picture issues, on the one hand, and a member of a tightly knit community intensely focused on the values and need of one's hometown, on the other hand, defines our age. It represents a source of energy that communities can tap into.

If you think you are too small to make a difference,
you have not been in bed with a mosquito.

— ANITA RODDICK

When the Kalamazoo Promise was announced, Southwest Michigan First immediately recognized a golden opportunity to promote the highly unusual economic development program well beyond the region. It hired Development Counsellors International, a New York City public relations firm, to launch an aggressive media relations campaign to get the word out. As a result, the program made front-page news in *The Wall Street Journal*, was featured on ABC News and CNN and grabbed headlines in *The New York Times*, *The Washington Post*, *The Chicago Tribune* and a number of other national newspapers and magazines. Most recently, Katie Couric's five-minute segment on the Kalamazoo Promise for the CBS Evening News was invaluable; the adage indeed is the best advertisement is the one you get where someone positively mentions your name and you didn't even have to pay for it. Kalamazoo's appeal as a business location was no longer a best-kept secret and the city's turnaround got another strong shot in the arm.

With the steady drumbeat of positive press, Kalamazoo attracted the attention of the editors at *Fast Company* magazine and the city became the first ever to be named to the publication's prestigious "Fast 50" list in 2007. Kalamazoo's signature business model of Community Capitalism also got its first mention by name.

As John F. Kennedy once said, "Change is the law of life. And those who look only to the past or the present are certain to miss the future." In today's fiercely competitive, global battle for business, communities that are stuck in the old model for economic development will wither and die. Those that embrace change and initiate their own version of Community Capitalism – in whatever form it might take – are on the road to relevancy and being able to compete in this century.

Community Capitalism isn't simply about applying the tactics of the business world to community development, or about trying to infuse the values of philanthropy into corporations. It's a merger of the two, and recognition that each has something to offer the other. Kalamazoo has seen efforts to bring the best aspects of the private sector – the focus and reward for performance, the sense of accountability and an appreciation of the power of incentives – to bear on non-profit ventures. Bronson Methodist Hospital took the commitment to quality seen in the for-profit corporate world and applied it to its core operations of delivering health care. The Radisson Plaza Hotel, acquired with benevolent intent, needed to succeed as a business. The non-profit mindsets of cooperation, sharing of best practices and not seeing the world as a zero-sum arena have likewise permeated the mindset of many local corporations. It is evident, for example, in the community-wide adoption of a talent-driven model and in the collaborative efforts to seek new developments for downtown. It is also revealed in the Southwest Michigan First Life Science Fund, which layers a strong sense of community interest on top of the intense rigors of venture capital. "When philanthropy and business investment occur together, there's a multiplier effect," said Bill Johnston, "and if it is focused and organized, it is Community Capitalism."

When philanthropy and business investment occur together, there's a multiplier effect, and if it is focused and organized, it is Community Capitalism.

– BILL JOHNSTON

While Kalamazoo's economic development model of Community Capitalism grew up organically, piece by piece as needs arose, it now serves as the basis for our future – and can too for yours. We have lived through its birth and now know how to hone its "pieces." We continually scrutinize each challenge that we face to see if we have a puzzle piece to address it. And, we are careful to look outside our front door to other places around the world to study how others use components of our model and consider new suggestions to help us address rising needs.

Kalamazoo's Community Capitalism model is unlike other economic models because the Kalamazoo community knows that it is never "done." It is a puzzle where the pieces need to be picked up and tried and fit in different ways over and over in order to make the best fit. Communities must always be on the lookout for a piece that may have dropped on the floor and needs to be "fit" in. Like Kalamazoo, business leaders, government officials and economic developers need to be ready to change and adapt as future economic conditions and challenges arise in order to achieve their ultimate goal – job and wealth creation.

EPILOGUE:
COMMUNITY CAPITALISM

THE CHALLENGE

Community and economic growth is often discussed in terms of sole strategies. These strategies are often based on the latest perceived fad. While the majority of these strategies are correct, they were never intended to be singular solutions to growing and developing an economy.

THE RESPONSE

Community Capitalism, using Kalamazoo, Michigan as the primary example along with stories from around the world, represents 20 years of study and observations about what the crucial elements of successful regions are and how those elements are delivered.

THE FINDINGS

Community Capitalism will surprise many with its simplicity and how easy it can be for nearly every community around the globe to achieve success with this approach. The stories contained within the book demonstrate that a community need not have access to great wealth to succeed, but only a commitment to success itself. The key findings of Community Capitalism include:

Place: More than any other time in history, people have the choice to live where their surroundings meet their cultural, civic and human needs. Increasingly, communities that succeed are those that develop a sense of place for those who currently live there, as well as those they hope to recruit.

Capital: It is about money. Companies cannot grow without it. People will move to access it. Communities that succeed will find ways to ensure that the flow of capital is maintained to meet the needs of individuals and companies.

Infrastructure: The infrastructure of growth is no longer water or sewer lines. Today, the infrastructure of growth is engineering schools, high-tech incubators and research institutions.

Talent: Gone are the days when advanced economies can focus on natural resources or low cost. The number one indicator of sustainable success is now the creation, development and deployment of talent.

Education: Great minds do great things. Communities that succeed will increasingly focus on access to education that is relevant, lifelong and delivered in a manner that encourages the recipient to make the community home for life.

Many of the findings of Community Capitalism fly in the face of those who want to believe that there is a "white knight" of an economic development strategy that will bring prosperity into their community. By investing in the five Community Capitalism strategies, communities will ensure their ability not only to prosper, but also to thrive in a changing economy.

ABOUT THE AUTHOR

Described by *The Economist* as "an energetic economic development leader," Ron Kitchens is the Chief Executive Officer of Southwest Michigan First, as well as the General Partner of the Southwest Michigan First Life Science Fund. Ron hosts a weekly television program, "Business First," authors a bimonthly business column and speaks to business and professional groups throughout the nation.

Throughout his nearly 25-year career in economic development in Michigan, Texas and Missouri, Ron has worked with more than 200 Fortune 500, international or regional corporations as diverse as Citi Group, GE Capital, Aker, Celanese, Scholastic, Kiewit Offshore Services, Boeing, Exxon Mobil and Ryan Sanders Baseball.

In addition to his broad-based experience, Ron has successfully started and operated multiple privately held companies. He was elected as a city councilman at the age of 21 in his hometown of Ozark, Missouri and served as a staff member to United States Senator John Danforth. He is a graduate of Missouri State University.

Ron's work has been cited in *Fast Company*, *Forbes*, *The Wall Street Journal*, CBS News and National Public Radio, along with dozens of other national and international media outlets. His work also has been recognized with dozens of awards, including the prestigious National Marketing for Results Award and the Leadership and Innovation Award from CoreNet Global.

*Our efforts to make a positive impact
in the world and in people's lives were not acts of charity,
but rather of enlightened self interest.*

— CARLY FIORINA

LaVergne, TN USA
20 August 2010
193922LV00006B/14/P